CAPTAIN
from
Fundy

CAPTAIN
from
Fundy

THE LIFE AND TIMES
OF GEORGE D. SPICER,
MASTER OF SQUARE-
RIGGED WINDJAMMERS

Stanley T. Spicer

LANCELOT PRESS
HANTSPORT, NOVA SCOTIA

ISBN 0-88999-392-0
Published 1988

LANCELOT PRESS LIMITED
Hantsport, Nova Scotia
Office and production facilities on Hwy. No. 1, $\frac{1}{2}$ mile east of Hantsport.

4

Dedication

To Linda, John and Neil I dedicate this story of their heritage.

The Old Ships of Fundy

Master mariners whose ships once ploughed the Seven Seas —
Skilled in seamanship of iron — blood — and frame —
Making unwrit sagas in their challenge to the deep —
Gave the ports from which they hailed a lasting fame.
But the men like the white sails . . .
A memory and a name.

How alone seems the waters when the tide is at the flood,
No white sails on their bosom as of yore!
Oh, the silence of the shipyards where the builders wrought
On the river banks and Minas Basin shore!
For the wooden ships with white sails
Pass to and fro no more.

A.J. Reynolds

Contents

Acknowledgements

I am deeply indebted to those institutions and individuals who, in various ways, contributed so much to this work.

The Archives, Dalhousie University Library; the Maritime Museum of the Atlantic; the Nova Scotia Public Archives, all of Halifax; and the Yarmouth County Museum, Yarmouth, Nova Scotia, provided factual material from their resources.

Mr. and Mrs. Bill Spicer and Mrs. Percy B. Spicer of Windsor, Ontario, generously loaned numerous original documents pertaining to Captain Spicer's career, and J.L. Maxwell Spicer of Spencers Island furnished information on original land grants in Spencers Island.

Then there were those who shared their memories of Captain Spicer: Eugene Spicer, Don Mills, Ontario; Mrs. Georgia Proctor, Spencers Island; Walter Allen, Amherst, Nova Scotia; Captain Wilson Morris and William Dunbar of Advocate, Nova Scotia; and Mrs. Clifford Dunbar, Mrs. Edgar Currie and H.A. (Sandy) Dunbar, all of Spencers Island. David Spicer, Delta, British Columbia, provided information on flying schedules which appears later in the work.

Finally, I acknowledge with special thanks the work of my wife Gwen, who spent countless hours checking facts and figures in proofreading; and of my daughter Linda MacDonald of Calgary, who typed the original manuscript.

S.T.S.

Illustrations

Brigantine *Amazon*, later mystery vessel *Mary Celeste* (Courtesy N.B. Museum)

Brig *Globe* (Courtesy the author)

Barque *J.F. Whitney* (Courtesy the author)

Ship *E.J. Spicer* (Courtesy the author)

Ship *Charles S. Whitney* (Courtesy the author)

Ship *Glooscap* in Tacoma (Courtesy Conrad Byers)

Barquentine *Perfection* (Courtesy Mrs. Emily Currie)

George D. and Emily Jane Spicer (Courtesy the author)

Crew of the Ship *Glooscap* (Courtesy Conrad Byers)

Shareholders, Spencers Island Company (Courtesy the author)

Spencers Island Shipyard (Courtesy Conrad Byers)

Three-Masted Schooner Under Sail (Courtesy Conrad Byers)

Glossary

Able Seaman (A.B.): an able or experienced seaman of proven competence.

Chronometer: an accurate timepiece used for navigational purposes.

Clear: authority for a vessel to leave or clear a port.

Drivers: in the context of this work, men who drove their vessels to get the last possible knot of speed without endangering vessel or crew.

Enter: registering a vessel's arrival in port.

Fathom: a unit of length or depth: six feet.

Forecastle (or fo'c'sle): accommodations forward for the crew.

Goose Wing: when only one corner of a close-reefed square sail is exposed to the wind; used in heavy wind conditions.

Heave-To: to stop a vessel or to control her with little or no forward movement.

In Irons: handcuffed; a sailor in irons was locked up in isolation.

Jury Rig: temporary repairs following damage at sea; e.g. a dismasting.

Knot: a speed of one nautical mile per hour.

Line: Equator; e.g. crossed the Line in Longitude 20⁰W.

Log: i. an instrument which measures distance travelled through the water. ii. to accomplish a speed or distance; e.g. She logged 200 miles. iii. a journal in which are recorded all important events concerning a vessel and her complement while at sea.

Master Mariner: synonymous with captain or master.

Nautical Mile: 6,080 feet as compared to a land mile of 5,280 feet.

Ordinary Seaman: a novice or inexperienced seaman.

Palm: a leather hand band used when sewing canvas.

Passage: a voyage from one port to another.

Pooped: a sea breaking over the stern of a vessel.

Rigging: a general term for all the wire and ropes fitted to stay the masts and to work the yards and sails.

Scurvy: a disease caused by a lack of ascorbic acid.

Shipwright: a carpenter skilled in the technique of shipbuilding.

Sojering: loafing or performing work half-heartedly.

Square-Rigger: a vessel with sails set on yards crosswise to the fore and aft line of the hull.

Tack: to bring a vessel's bow across the wind to change direction.

Tonnage: the cubic capacity of a vessel: one hundred cubic feet equals one ton.

Vessel: a general term applied to craft but excluding small boats; does not refer to a particular rig as does brig, barque, etc.

Wear Ship: to bring a vessel on the other tack by swinging her stern across the wind.

Yards: spars fastened at their centres to a mast upon which square sails are attached.

Rigs

Barque (or Bark): a vessel with three or more masts, carrying square sails on all but the after mast which carries fore and aft sails. See photo barque *J.F. Whitney.*

Barquentine (or Barkentine): a vessel with three or more masts, carrying square sails only on the foremast and fore and aft sails on all other masts. See photo barqentine *Perfection.*

Brig: a two-masted vessel with square sails on each mast. See photo brig *Globe.*

Brigantine: a two-masted vessel with square sails on the foremast and fore and aft sails on the mainmast. See photo brigantine *Amazon.*

Schooner: a fore and aft rigged vessel with two or more masts. See photo of schooner.

Ship: a vessel with three or more masts carrying square sails on all masts. See photos *Charles S. Whitney* or *E.J. Spicer.*

Tern schooner: a three-masted schooner.

Foreword

I still have vivid memories of Captain George D. Spicer. When he died in 1937 at the age of ninety-one, I was a young teenager, and many times over the years I have thought of the great changes that have come about during our overlapping lives.

George Spicer was a boy during the Crimean War, he witnessed a portion of the American Civil War and had an involvement in the Spanish-American War. He would live through the First World War and most of the Great Depression.

In his time much of the world would be taken from the candle to the kerosene lamp by Abraham Gesner and, later, Spicer would come to know electricity, the telephone, radio, the automobile and the aeroplane. If, as a young captain, George Spicer was used to dealing in Nova Scotia currency he would, in time, become familiar with the Canadian dollar.

After his death, but in my lifetime, the world has moved on to television, computers, the atomic and nuclear age, and walks on the moon. Those of my generation have known the Second World War, Korea, Vietnam, the Cold War and decades of an uneasy peace, living always with the knowledge that the next global conflict could well be the last. One can wonder what thoughts would come to the person of today if he or she was suddenly transplanted back to the 1850s, or if the child of the 1850s was placed in today's world. Undoubtedly neither would be very comfortable, at least for awhile.

In his late years, George Spicer still stood a full six feet in height and, if age had wasted some of the flesh from a two-hundred pound frame, he retained the very large hands common to many seamen of his time. He had a soft baritone voice but, if he was aroused, one could easily imagine that voice carrying above the sounds of wind and waves. Always he wore the mutton chop whiskers with the clean-shaven chin, and several times each day he would carefully brush his whiskers. A small mirror and brush were kept near his desk for that purpose.

The captain was a man of precise habits. He rose daily at 6:00 a.m. made the kitchen fire and had tea at 7:00. Breakfast was served at eight o'clock and another cup of tea at 10:30. The main meal of the day was at noon, followed by a nap on the kitchen couch and a cup of tea at two. Supper was a light meal, followed by his one cigar of the day. His tea had to be boiling hot; flavour was not so important, but woe betide anyone serving him a lukewarm cup of tea. He always had his own pot of molasses by his place at the head of the table. If someone else wanted molasses, it was brought in a separate container. His was sacred to himself.

George Spicer was never known to swear. His strongest epithet was O Pshaw! He did not drink and, above all, he could not stand anyone whistling within his hearing. Perhaps it was a carry-over from his years at sea when whistling aboard ship was thought by many to bring bad luck.

In religion he was Baptist and, if he was known to regularly fall asleep in church, he could invariably quote Chapter and Verse of the sermon's text following the service. Always a Conservative, he corresponded with many of the political leaders of the day — as long as they were Conservative.

Spicer was a great reader, preferring biographies and books by the religious leaders of the time. Napoleon was a favourite figure, as were Livingstone and Stanley, the African explorers. One of his favourite pastimes was euchre, and frequently he closed the day's entry in his diary with the phrase, 'We had a game.'

He liked to have children around but did not like to see boys with time on their hands, and he always found something for them to do: carrying wood, cleaning out the stable or brushing down the horse. Always he kept a diary. Even on the day he died, he made a few unintelligible scratches for his daily entry. A new diary and a box of cigars were mandatory Christmas gifts, everything else was secondary.

In his later years, George Spicer's birthdays on September 8 were occasions for family get-togethers. There might be fifteen or more of different generations present to celebrate, and the old man displayed a touch of sentimentality for, before parting, he would always ask them to sing "God Be With You Till We Meet Again." When it was sung at his last few birthdays, there were numerous moist eyes.

Before and throughout his retirement years, the captain had a horse. The last was a white horse named Andy, acquired in 1917, and he stayed around until the mid-1930s. Andy gained a measure of local fame for having a mind of his own. There was a small pasture with a pole gate adjoining the barn. When Andy was in the pasture and developed wanderlust, which was often, he would carefully remove the poles with his teeth and go for a walk. Sometimes he would come back on his own. If a local boy was brushing him down and Andy was not satisfied with the method, he would gently sidle over to the side of the stall, pinning the boy — not hard, just enough to give him a message. And Andy liked to try out new people — especially boys. If he was harnessed to a wagon with a boy manning the reins and Andy decided he was tired, he would come to a halt and nothing would make him move until he was ready. Andy did not try that with the captain.

One day one of the local lads badly wanted to rent Andy to go to nearby Advocate. The going fee was one dollar but the boy had no money. He approached Captain Spicer and a deal was arranged whereby the boy would work off the dollar after school and on Saturdays. Following several weeks of diligently adhering to the schedule, the young fellow decided he had more than made up the dollar. He carefully approached the captain and, after a moment's pondering, the old mariner allowed that perhaps the debt was paid in full. There was a twinkle in his eye when he rendered the decision, but if the lad had not had the courage to make his move, he could have worked weeks longer.

There was one overriding and consistent characteristic of Captain Spicer, and it was his firm belief that there was a place for everything and everything in its place. It was undoubtedly another habit carried over from his life on board ship. If a book was removed from the bookcase, it was to be placed back in the bookcase. If a broom or garden implement was not put back in its proper location, the guilty party would be quietly reminded of the way things were done about the captain's property.

But all of this tells something of the man in the late years of his life. There is a beginning to the story of the life and times of George Dimock Spicer . . .

Stanley T. Spicer
Spencers Island, Nova Scotia

1

In The Beginning

*T*he two arms of the upper reaches of the Bay of Fundy bore far into the Province of Nova Scotia. One arm nearly separates the province from the rest of Canada, while the other arm culminates in the Minas Basin. Standing like a sentinel at the juncture of these two arms is Cape Chignecto and south along the cape flow the waters of Minas Channel leading into the Basin of Minas, nearly thirty miles to the east.

It is not known for certain who among the early explorers first cast their eyes on this rugged land. The Bretons and the men of Normandy were fishing on the Grand Banks and along the coasts of Newfoundland in the sixteenth century and it is quite possible that some of these adventurers may well have sailed along the coast of Nova Scotia and into the Bay of Fundy.

The first recorded exploration of the territory was by Samuel de Champlain in 1604 and in succeeding years when he, along with DeMonts, Poutrincourt and their company sailed up the headwaters of the Bay of Fundy. They gave names to and left detailed descriptions of such landmarks as Cape Chignecto, Ile Haute, Cape D'Or and Advocate. One of the fascinating discoveries documented was the finding of an old iron cross implanted near the mouth of Parrsboro Harbour.

The origin of the cross has never been firmly established but it lends some credence to a theory advanced by writer

Frederick Pohl that Prince Henry Sinclair of the Orkney Islands not only explored the area near the close of the fourteenth century but that he wintered on Cape D'Or. According to Pohl, the accounts of Sinclair's travels minutely describe the land around Minas Basin as well as what are now parts of Pictou and Guysborough counties. Pohl further contends that Prince Henry was the father-figure for the great god-man, Glooscap.

It is a storied land this Parrsboro shore. It knew Indian encampments and the settlement of Acadians. It witnessed vessels sailing past its shore during the innumerable wars between France and England. Remains of uncounted soldiers, settlers and Indians rest within its soil.

Here the story of George Dimock Spicer unfolds, but its real beginnings go across the Atlantic Ocean to Wales. In the middle years of the eighteenth century, a wealthy Welsh family named Chomondelay had in their employ a young coachman named Robert Spicer. An Englishman whose own history is obscure but whose ancestors were dealers in spices, Spicer did not enjoy a high station in Welsh social life.

Within the Chomondelay family was a daughter, Priscilla, and in the course of time she and Robert fell in love. Permission to marry was flatly rejected so the couple promptly eloped to North America. Priscilla was just as promptly disinherited.

Robert enlisted in the New Jersey Volunteers fighting on the side of the British during the American Revolution and won his commission in the field as lieutenant. Following the end of the Revolution, Robert and his family came to Nova Scotia to take possession of the five hundred acres he had been granted as a Loyalist in August 1785. The land was located at Spencers Island, on the north shore of Minas Channel, in the Township of Parrsborough. At some point, Priscilla's parents realized that the marriage was secure and sent over furniture and silver as her dowry.

The family's first home in this new land was a rough log cabin. These early years were difficult, especially for Priscilla. She was a woman born into a life of wealth and ease, living in a small cabin in a clearing with only the animals of the forest for company. But she never wavered.

Four sons and two daughters were born of the marriage and when the oldest son, also Robert, reached adulthood, he was given the homestead. The rest of the family moved a few miles west to Advocate, the site of an old Acadian settlement, where Robert and Priscilla lived out the rest of their lives.

In 1809, the year before his death, the senior Robert made his will. It is characteristic of the times in the way it specifies the care that was to be attended his wife. In part it reads, in the original spelling:

> John Spicer shall pay and provide for his Dere mother until Joseph is twenty-one years of age and then they two shall pay equelly alike their mother as followes and that to be continued durin her natural life. The following articals, one comfortable room in the hous and firewood for one fire cut at the dore with her bead and furniture to make her comfortable. Fore hundred wate of good flower, two hundred wate of good pork, sixty wate of fresh beef or mutton, forty bushels of potaters put in the sellor. Also the use of one cowe, it to bee kept summer and winter and to be drove to her dore at night in the summer time. Also six pounde of wool, ten poundes of flax, two pare of shoes, six poundes of candels and her bill to be paid at the store.

Priscilla lived for ten years on the provisions in her husband's will before passing away in 1820 at the age of seventy-five.

The younger Robert farmed the homestead and apparently was an astute businessman. He gradually acquired land from adjoining grantees until he owned upwards of twenty-five hundred acres. On his death in 1859, the property passed to two of his sons, Isaac and Jacob.

Jacob married Mary Reid and the couple had eleven children, two of whom died in childhood. Of the remaining nine, the four sons would become master mariners while two of the daughters would marry sea captains and each would lose her first husband at sea.

George D. Spicer, the eldest child of Jacob and Mary, was born on September 8, 1846. As a young boy, he was required to do his share of work about the farm but his heart was not in it. His eyes were on the waters of the Bay of Fundy and his dreams on the seas beyond. At the age of twelve he embarked on a seafaring career which would encompass the next fifty-two years. New York would be his home port and the oceans of the world his highway. When his years of sailing the seas were over he would come home to Spencers Island for good. Over the years George would be followed at sea by his three younger brothers: Johnson, Dewis and Edmund. All began under sail and all stayed in sail. The steam-powered vessels were not for them.

2
Early Years at Sea

*T*he dawn of shipbuilding in Canada's Maritime provinces coincided with the earliest settlements for in those days there were no roads; the sea was the highway and from the first, fish was a basic commodity for food and for trade. If money was scarce, the forest was at the settlers' doorsteps and it provided the raw materials for building vessels as well as cargoes for export. From the beginning these provinces bred men who could fell the trees, build their vessels and sail them across the seas. The influx of thousands of Loyalists in the later years of the eighteenth century brought many men who were skilled shipwrights and merchants to add impetus to the infant industry.

By the 1850s shipbuilding was well established along the shores and rivers of all three provinces. The discovery of gold in Australia in 1851 provided an important new stimulus to Maritime shipbuilders as, suddenly, the established shipyards in Britain and the United States were unable to meet the instant demand for fast vessels to carry the thousands of adventurers clamoring to get to the gold fields. Some shipyards, notably in Saint John, were quick to rise to the challenge and clippers like the *Marco Polo* and *Star of the East* came out of the old port city to take their places among the world's fastest vessels of their time. In 1858 over 2,100 deep-water vessels were owned in Nova Scotia alone while New Brunswick and Prince Edward Island were keeping pace.

In these years aspiring young merchant sailors from the Maritime provinces did not attend marine academies nor did they sign on training ships. Their apprenticeships were served in the fo'c'sles of fishing schooners, small coasters or deep-water vessels. They shipped out 'before the mast' and if a kindly captain or mate deigned to take a young boy in hand and teach him some of the skills of seamanship so much the better. But first, last and always it was up to the boy to prove he had the aptitude and toughness to be a sailor and, perhaps later, an officer. Those who lacked either capacity or who were deemed lazy soon found themselves back on land and glad of it. It was a hard school.

The experienced seaman on a sailing vessel was a man of many talents. He had to be able to steer — to keep a vessel on her course in all kinds of wind and sea conditions, to handle heavy canvas sails far above the deck whether in the calms of the tropics or on wildly swaying spars while the vessel below him pitched and rolled on the wintry North Atlantic. He had to know how to sew for the repair of old sails and making new sails was a constant job at sea. On the square-rigged vessels there were dozens of lines, each with its own specific function and the seaman had to know them all on the blackest of nights or when the decks were awash with green water. Always there were spars to scrape, wood to paint and rigging to splice or tar. And the man who failed to do his job quickly and efficiently soon knew the wrath of the officers. The Maritime shipmaster and his officers wore no uniform but almost without exception they were sticklers for discipline. They demanded the smart handling of smart vessels and anyone violating the code was brought into line quickly and, if necessary, forcibly.

Thus is was in June 1858 when twelve-year-old George Spicer signed on his first vessel, the schooner *Emma Johnston*, a coaster plying between Bay of Fundy ports. Over the next three years he served on several vessels of various rigs and then, in 1861, Spicer signed on the brigantine *Amazon*, newly launched at Spencers Island. Eleven years later the brigantine, renamed the *Mary Celeste*, became one of the most renowned vessels of all time when she was found sailing off the Azores without a soul on board. What happened to her captain, his wife, their two-year-old daughter and the crew of seven is a question which has remained unanswered to this day.

But after her launching in 1861, with George Spicer a member of her crew, the brigantine sailed up the Bay of Fundy to Five Islands to load lumber for England. Her captain, young Robert McLellan from nearby Economy, had been but recently married. During the vessel's loading, McLellan was far from well but determined to make the voyage. The *Amazon* sailed from Five Islands but while still in the Bay of Fundy Captain McLellan became seriously ill with pneumonia and the vessel was put about. The captain was landed at Spencers Island where he died a few hours later at the Spicer home. The next day some of the crew wrapped the captain's body in a blanket, placed it in the *Amazon's* boat and sailed to Economy. As they approached the shore at Economy the young bride of Captain McLellan came running to learn why they had returned. It was a sight George Spicer never forgot.

Spicer went on to other vessels while continuing to learn his trade and began sailing to various European ports. The year 1863 found him back in North America, in Baltimore, where he signed as second mate on an American vessel, the *Julia A. Whitford*. The records are fragmentary but there is evidence that the vessel was engaged in carrying troops to the James River in Virginia during the American Civil War. In later years Spicer referred to the *Whitford* as an American transport and wrote of being on the James River. It is more than likely that he witnessed some of the fighting between the armies of Generals Ulysses S. Grant and Robert E. Lee in the year prior to the burning of Richmond.

By 1868 Spicer had spent ten years on vessels of various sizes and rigs. He had served his time, learned his trade and was now an experienced mate. But before he wrote the Board of Trade examinations for his master's ticket there was a matter of even more immediate priority — his marriage.

If the practical aspects of seamanship were learned in the demanding school of the fo'c'sle, those young men aspiring to command still had to acquire formal training in navigation and for this purpose classes were conducted in many of the coastal towns and villages. Early in his career George recognized this need in his education and he interrupted his seafaring activities to come back to Advocate where a local teacher was instilling the theory and practice of navigation into the minds of hopeful, future sea captains. The second day in class he saw a young girl with blonde, reddish hair walking by and many years later he remembered saying to himself, 'There goes my wife.' The girl was Emily Jane Morris, also of Loyalist stock, and after a courtship sandwiched between voyages he proved himself a good prophet for on August 6, 1868 George D. Spicer and Emily Jane Morris were married.

The young couple proceeded to Liverpool, England, where in October 1868 George passed his examinations for master. He was immediately offered command of the 289 ton brig, *Globe*, the first of the five vessels Spicer would command over the next forty-two years.

Emily sailed with her husband almost constantly except when she came ashore to have children. Their honeymoon voyage was to the far east but for the most part, the years on the *Globe* were spent on transatlantic runs between New York and London or Liverpool.

In these early years George was receiving fifty dollars a month in wages plus six per cent on the money he remitted as profits to the vessel's owners. If this appears as small remuneration for the captain of a vessel, it must be balanced against the living costs of the time. In Halifax, molasses sold for 38¢ a gallon, sugar was 8¢ a pound, tea 40¢ a pound and a barrel of flour could be purchased for $6.25.

The *Globe* was the only vessel he commanded in which George Spicer did not own shares. Ownership in nearly all the square-riggers and schooners built in the Maritime provinces was based upon sixty-four equal shares. While one man or a firm might own a vessel outright, more often ownership was spread among a number of shareholders. Thus a vessel's costs, profits and any losses were shared among the owners. In later years George Spicer owned shares in all of the vessels he commanded as well as in other vessels. Some years there were losses but on balance the returns from these shares formed an important part of his livelihood.

As master of the *Globe*, Captain George Spicer joined a company of hundreds of master mariners with many common characteristics. Nearly all had gone to sea at an early age so possessed little formal education. If their training in navigation was limited, they still managed to take their vessels to destinations all over the world and bring them back again. And they were superb seamen, able handlers of their vessels and the crews they commanded. This latter trait was particularly important in the late years of sail when many of the best seamen were going into steam and the windships were often left with the human dregs of the ports.

At sea the captain led a lonely life, one of the main reasons so many took their wives and families whenever possible. He would work alongside the men, painting, splicing or sewing sails but he was the supreme authority on board ship and his word was law. The sailors lived forward, the officers lived aft and the captain lived essentially by himself.

But there was more to a sea captain's responsibilities than handling the vessel and crew at sea. In port he had to negotiate tugboat fees, enter and clear his vessel, select and purchase stores and, sometimes, arrange for the loading and unloading of cargoes. Occasionally it was left to the captain to find charters. Always charterers were seeking the lowest possible freight rates and always the vessel's owners were seeking profitable rates. The successful captain had need of a keen business sense and sharp negotiating skills to go with his seagoing talents. Then, if his vessel needed repairs it was up to the captain to arrange drydocking and to ensure that the work was properly completed at a fair price.

This then was the kind of life that George D. Spicer embarked upon when he took command of the *Globe* that October day in 1868. He would live out the next four decades in much the same way as countless other shipmasters of his time but he would come to know adventures, triumphs and heartbreaks of his own.

3
A Launching

*S*ome years after he retired from the sea, George Spicer looked back over his records and found he had crossed the Atlantic 107 times in his seafaring career. In our present age of jet travel, when each crossing is only a matter of hours, this would not be a particularly significant accomplishment. But in his time, in the old windships, each crossing could take a month or more and few were the crossings not beset by gales, hurricanes, heavy seas or headwinds. If, in the glorious days of the clipper ships, the *Red Jacket* could sail from New York to Liverpool, England in twelve days, the windjammers from the Maritime provinces making the same passage in sixteen days were considered exceedingly fast.

Captain Spicer remained in the *Globe* until 1872 when the vessel was sold. He returned to Spencers Island where a new barque of 701 tons was nearing completion and she was to be under his command. The barque was named the *J.F. Whitney* after the New York firm which was beginning an active interest in most of the vessels built at Spencers Island. The company would not only have a financial interest in these vessels, it would also manage them and, because of this affiliation, New York would become their home port. And, beginning with the *J.F. Whitney*, Spicer became a part-owner of all the vessels he sailed and, with the managing firm, would be heavily involved with the business aspects of operating square-riggers.

It was in the *J.F. Whitney* that Spicer began to earn his reputation as a driver. In the years between 1873 and 1878 the *Whitney* was credited with an average passage on North Atlantic voyages of twenty-one days to the eastward and thirty-one days to the westward, a fact duly noted by a New York newspaper:

> **New York.** Fast sailing bark *J.F. Whitney*, Captain George D. Spicer in making ten successive voyages across the Atlantic — from ports in the United States to ports in the United Kingdom and the Continent — has made the unprecedented average time of 21 days to the eastward and 31 days to the westward. This for all seasons, winter included, may be called fast sailing. During all ten voyages underwriters on cargo or vessel have not been called upon to pay a dollar for damage.

It was while the *J.F. Whitney* was plying the North Atlantic that Nova Scotia reached its zenith in the building and owning of wooden windships. By 1874 the province would boast of 826 square-rigged vessels on her registers comprising 104 ships, 300 barques, 9 barquentines, 384 brigantines and 29 brigs, in addition to hundreds of sloops and schooners. By 1878, when Canada ranked fourth among the ship-owning nations of the world, Nova Scotia alone contributed nearly half of the country's total tonnage.

In these years shipyards ringed the coasts and rivers of Nova Scotia and the launching of a square-rigged vessel was always an event which attracted visitors from far and near. Indeed, four thousand had come to the village of Maitland to witness the launching of the big ship *W.D. Lawrence* in 1874. Such was their frequency, however, that launchings did not always command much newspaper space.

During the summer of 1876, Amasa Loomer, a prominent builder of Spencers Island vessels, had completed the 1,283 ton barque *Calcutta*. Her launching is rather unique in that there exists a detailed description as written by young Lester Dewis whose father, Captain Robert Dewis, would take command of the vessel:

On August 24, 1876 the barque *Calcutta* was launched from the shipyard of Payzant and Bigelow, Spencers Island, N.S. She was a three-decked vessel of 175 foot keel, about 40 foot beam and 25 foot depth of hold and registered 1283 tons net. She was a splendid vessel in every particular, well-built and finely finished with all the latest improvements of the date in the matter of sails, rigging and iron work.

The *Calcutta* was launched fully-rigged with colours flying and she made a beautiful exhibit of marine architecture as she slid gracefully into the blue waters of the Bay of Fundy. The side-wheel steamer, *G.A. Good* of Windsor, loaded with sightseers stood by to take her in tow to her anchorage but by the captain's orders, the mate assisted by a crowd of young boys, myself included, hoisted up the spanker, a topsail and the foremast staysail and she passed the steamer easily.

The launching brought a large crowd to enjoy the day and to see the sights. They walked or drove if they could from Truro, Amherst and up the Shulee shore. Those from the south shore of the Bay, from Scot's Bay down to Margaretsville came by boat and as already said, the *G.A. Good* carried a boat load from Windsor. All the Minas country was represented. There were more than a thousand visitors. Some carried lunch but the ladies of the place served dinners in the shipyard and lunch tables were set up. A great tea meeting went on in the afternoon. The tea meeting and refreshment booths cleared a lot of money and the proceeds went to the building of the Spencers Island Union Church.

The crowd was saddened by the drowning of a young man from Kingsport who fell overboard from the schooner *Mary Grace* of that place. However, old feuds along the shore were settled. It was realized that life is too short. Then everyone left for home with good feelings and thankful hearts.

To give some idea of the amount of work involved in building a vessel of this size from the growing tree to the floating ship, I will try to enumerate the different departments of work and the men in charge of each.

Gideon Bigelow of Canning made the model; the Spicers of Spencers Island supplied the timber; Joshua Dewis was responsible for all the correct parts; Amasa Loomer of Spencers Island was the master builder; Sidney Blenkhorn of Advocate supplied the iron and did the blacksmith work; James Nichols and Sons of Advocate made the blocks; George Cox of Canning, a joiner, made the cabins; Jim Longley of Canning did the ceilings and planking; Harris Brown of Advocate did the hole boring; Justin Bigelow of Kingsport did the caulking; John Barkhouse of Pereaux put in the iron knees; John Pettis of Port Greville built the boats; Tom Willigar of Black Rock built the ship's gig; Silas Armstrong of Avondale, Hants County was the rigger; John Allen of Windsor did the wood carving and there was a large amount on this vessel. She was the last vessel, I think on this side of the Bay of Fundy to have the carved figure of a woman for a figurehead; this one represented Queen Victoria.

The *Calcutta* was destined for a relatively short life. In 1883 she struck a coral reef in the Malacca Strait while enroute to Manila and had to be abandoned. Captain Dewis, his wife and the crew remained on the reef for three weeks fitting out one of the vessel's small boats. After seven days and nights of rough sailing they managed to reach Singapore and found passage home by way of India, the Suez Canal and London.

4

Mystery of the Lost Barque

A ugust 1877 found Captain Spicer in New York following a voyage from Rotterdam with a cargo of empty barrels. While the cargo was being unloaded, Spicer was summoned to sit on a Court of Inquiry to examine the circumstances surrounding the loss of a vessel named the *Berthe Et Marie* in the North Atlantic a few weeks earlier. Such inquiries were called whenever a vessel was lost and their purpose was to determine cause and to affix blame, if any. This court sat for three days, was briefly adjourned and then recalled when the captain of the vessel was suddenly accused of burning his ship. A New York newspaper of the day gave a long account of the incident:

> A special Naval Court has been in session for the past week at the office of the British Consul General, engaged in trying a case of more than ordinary interest and importance to shipping and commercial agents. The court was composed of E.M. Archibald, British Consul; William Rice Courtney, master of the bark *Inverness* of London and George D. Spicer, master of the bark *J.F. Whitney* of Nova Scotia and was assembled to inquire into the circumstances connected with the abandonment at sea on July 22 last of the bark *Berthe Et Marie* of Kingston, Jamaica while on her voyage from Port-au-Prince to Falmouth, with a valuable cargo of mahogany, rum and West Indian

spices. It was charged that Captain Del Fosse, the master of the vessel, had started from Port-au-Prince knowing that his vessel was not seaworthy, and that, when in mid-ocean, he had allowed her to become half-filled with water, and that he had deliberately set fire to her for the purpose of obtaining a reward for himself and to secure the vessel's insurance for her owners. The vessel left Port-au-Prince on June 29 last, the crew numbering 11 hands, including the master, mate, cook and steward and was supposed to be in first-class order. The clearance papers show she was not overloaded. Capt. Del Fosse before leaving port stated that the vessel had two full suits of sails but the testimony of the mate shows that she had only a portion of the second suit. All went well up to July 4, when the vessel had proceeded as far as Mague where she was struck by a storm and her main topgallant yard carried away. She then put into Jamaica Bay, Castle Island, where she remained for five days for the ostensible purpose of repairs. The repairing, some of the seamen assert, was done imperfectly. On July 11 she put to sea again and on the following day the first mate reported to the captain that she was leaking to such an extent that all hands had been placed at the pumps. The men worked hard for four hours but the water gained rapidly on them. On July 16 it was discovered that the depth of water in the hold was increasing at the rate of six or seven inches per hour. On July 19 she was found to be making 19 inches of water per hour and, as the men were exhausted, she was put about for the purpose of making an American port north of Hatteras. Very little progress was made, however, and early on the morning of July 22 she was found to be waterlogged and apparently sinking. Capt. Del Fosse gave orders to launch the boats when about 120 miles from the nearest land. The mate, with five of the seamen, left in the long boat which was fully provisioned, and was followed about an hour afterward by the captain and the remainder of the crew in another boat. The boats kept together the whole of that day, steering northwest but during the next night they were separated. The boat containing the captain and his portion of the crew reached New York safely three days later. The long boat was picked up by the bark *Rio* on July 23, and her crew were taken to Deboy, Georgia from which point they came to New York. This portion of the story is corroborated by M. Victor Duzant, the mate of the vessel, and by all of the crew at present in the city.

The principal witness against the captain was Alexander Douglass, who resides at No. 219 Rutledge Street, Williamsburg. He testified that on July 27 Capt. Del Fosse went to his office and said he had lost his bark. When asked 'How did you come to lose her?' he laughed and said, 'I got pretty well paid for it.' The witness said 'You have got paid for it, eh, what kind of pay?' The captain answered, 'About $5,000, is that enough?' When asked to state what he had done to the vessel the captain said, 'In the first place, when I left Port-au-Prince my vessel was in a leaky condition and her pumps were in bad order. I got as far as the Bahama Islands, and there I fixed up the rigging a bit, and went on until I got abreast of Cape Hatteras, where, as she was leaking badly, I left her. I fixed my men alright and then put them in the boats and pulled off. Then, to make the thing sure, I went to the vessel again and stove in 24 puncheons of rum, and got all the oil I could find in the vessel and saturated the deck and then set her on fire. Then we left her, and I stood off for three or four hours to see her burn; I waited until I saw her masts fall and that was enough to satisfy me.' The witness continued that just at this point he noticed his son William Douglass had entered the office and that the captain at once stopped, and when the intruder had withdrawn asked the question. 'Do you think he heard what I said?' The captain also showed him a Bank of England note of the value of £500 which he said was part of his pay for the transaction; the same evening the witness' son told him he had overheard a part of the conversation and told him that it was his duty to report the matter to the authorities; he hesitated about doing so, but finally communicated with Capt. Brackett of the United States Secret Service and with Messrs. Mackie and Son, Lloyd's agents. William Douglass, the witness' son, corroborated his father's statements and testified that he distinctly heard the captain say that he fired the ship.

On behalf of the Captain, Duzant, the mate of the vessel and the other seamen swear positively that the captain and his portion of the crew left the vessel within half an hour after the long boat and did not return to the vessel. Captain Del Fosse also produced a long list of credentials from shipowners and merchants as to his character. The court decided if there was any ground for a charge it would have to be a criminal one, and that as it was a British vessel and the Captain a British subject, it would have to be conducted on British soil. They delivered a long opinion but declined to express any opinion as to the criminality of the master of the vessel.

Whether or not Captain Del Fosse was subsequently charged on his home soil is unknown but this account does provide a rather vivid picture of the kinds of incidents that came before Courts of Inquiry.

Captain Spicer's own notes of the sessions state that the captain was severely censured for not making greater efforts to save his vessel. Such verdicts were carefully noted by shipowners and insurance companies and could be decisive factors when shipmasters were being considered to command vessels.

A few days after the conclusion of the Court of Inquiry Spicer stepped back in time for a few hours. One of his old vessels, the brigantine *Amazon*, now *Mary Celeste*, was in port. Once again he walked the decks of the vessel, world famous after the disappearance of her complement, and the thoughts that crossed his mind will never be known. But if the *Mary Celeste* had achieved fame, she had also acquired notoriety as an unlucky vessel. Seamen were loathe to sail on her and she continually lost money for her owners until 1885 when she drove on a reef off Haiti. Years later another famous

Nova Scotian vessel would end her days not far from the *Mary Celeste*, the schooner *Bluenose*.

5

A Storm in Port

*V*essels sailing the North Atlantic in the fall and winter months usually encountered a full measure of adverse weather conditions. In October 1877 the *J.F. Whitney* sailed from Havre, France in ballast for New York. Almost immediately the barque ran into gale-force winds and high seas. Captain Spicer's entry in his diary for one day was typical of much of the voyage:

> **November 9** — At 7 a.m. wind hauled W.N.W. and N.W. in the squalls. Very heavy squalls all day attended with rain and hail in great quantities. A tremendous sea running N.W. and the vessel rolling and laboring much. Vessel laying to under two goose-winged topsails.

Then a few days later another entry:

> **November 15** — At noon Hans Anderson, A.B. of Hamburg, age 22 years fell from the upper fore topsail yard and broke his skull over his left temple so the brain protruded. He lived 1 3/4 hours. He had loosed the yard arm of the topsail and part of the weather side when he fell. I think the sail must have hit his feet and knocked him off. We sewed him up in canvas and put stones at his feet. Set the ensign at half mast.

At 4:30 p.m. we buried Hans Anderson. I read the burial service over him with all hands standing around with heads uncovered. Such is life. A very solemn sight to witness and to think about being ushered into Eternity without a moment's notice or preparation.

A storm at sea is one thing. At least there is usually sea room and plenty of water under the keel. A storm in port is an entirely different matter with other vessels in close proximity, land on two or three sides and various man-made obstacles such as docks and bridges nearby. It is a setting ready-made to breed catastrophe.

On January 11, 1879 the *J.F. Whitney* arrived in Bordeaux, France from New York with a cargo of naptha and crude oil. The cargo was unloaded and ballast taken on. The vessel was nearly ready to sail for New York when a storm struck the port. Captain Spicer described the events:

February 20 — This day a violent gale southwest and W.S.W. At noon the gale hauled northwest with terrific squalls, some rain and the very worst of weather. We had 75 fathoms of chain on one anchor and 30 on the other. We held on but the vessel rolled and tumbled about and I did not know what minute the chains would part and we would be adrift. Between noon and 1 p.m. the barque *Mary Stewart* left and we did not see her after. Suppose she parted her chains and drifted up the river. Another ship dragged about a mile and a steamer lost an anchor nearby.

It was an anxious day for all on board the *Whitney* and would have been even more so if they had known what was learned the following day. When the starboard anchor was hauled on board the stock was gone. Disaster may have been close at hand.

The incident was reminiscent of another vessel in another port some thirty years before which involved Captain David Cook of Yarmouth, N.S. In November 1849, while master of the little barque *Sarah*, Cook had rescued more than 350 passengers from the burning emigrant ship *Caleb*

Grimshaw enroute from Liverpool to New York. With such a crowd on board, there was no room for them below and most had to stay on deck in the frigid November weather. The *Sarah* was only provisioned for her own small complement and her stores could not last long even on the shortest of rations. Cook headed the *Sarah* for the nearest port, Horta in the Azores. The barque arrived there six days later, six days in which the exhausted, hungry emigrants had subsisted on a daily allowance of half a pint of water and half a biscuit morning and night.

The rescue of so many men, women and children on rough seas had been a harrowing experience in itself but in Horta, Captain Cook faced even more difficult problems. Port authorities ruled that the *Sarah*, like any vessel, must remain in quarantine for five days regardless of her crowded conditions. Only after the most strenuous entreaties was Captain Cook able to obtain permission for many of his passengers to be transferred ashore. Even so, more than one hundred were still on the *Sarah* when the wind blew up to a gale. A second anchor was set, then a third but the barque began to drag them all. Cook could do nothing more but watch as his vessel crept ever closer to the shore. The cable on one anchor snapped but the other two held as the *Sarah* was blown relentlessly towards the breakers, now visible even in the blackness of the night.

David Cook fully expected to lose his vessel and all on board and had told his passengers to prepare themselves. Then, in the last few moments before disaster struck, there was a lull and the wind swung around to the west. The *Sarah* was saved — but barely. The next morning when the anchors were hove up, the crew found both flukes on one had been broken off. Their lives had been saved by a single anchor.

6

A New Vessel and Loss of a Friend

*B*y 1880 George Spicer had been in command of the *J.F. Whitney* for nearly eight years. A new and much larger vessel was on the stocks at Spencers Island and Spicer was to take command. He turned the *Whitney* over to his brother Dewis in New York and returned home where he helped to complete the new vessel.

The ship *E.J. Spicer*, measuring 1,317 registered tons, was launched on November 17, 1880. Although Spicer commanded the ship for only five years, he always spoke of the 'E.J.' with particular affection. Perhaps it was because she was named after his wife, Emily Jane.

Captain Spicer sailed the new ship to Norfolk, Virginia where she was chartered to load cotton and lumber for Liverpool, England. It was in Norfolk that Spicer learned of the tragedy that had befallen his old friend, Captain Hiram Coalfleet.

George Spicer and Hiram Coalfleet had been friends for years. They frequently met in various ports, visited one another's vessels and together spent time on shore in these ports.

The story of Hiram Coalfleet had its beginnings many years before when a baby drifted ashore from a collier wrecked on the coast of Nova Scotia. Unknown and unnamed, the baby was taken in by a kindly family and given the name Coalfleet. From him was descended Hiram who, in the course of time, followed the sea and became a master mariner. In the late 1860s Captain Coalfleet was in command of the barque *Providence*, so-named because a disastrous fire had swept Canning, Nova Scotia in July 1866 while the vessel was still on the stocks and she escaped with only a scorched hull. While in the *Providence*, Captain Coalfleet was involved in a rescue of his own. It concerned a small schooner named *Industry*.

On December 11, 1868 the *Industry* left the LaHave River for Halifax only fifty-four miles distant. On board were the Captain, Lewis Sponagle; the vessel's owner, Ronald Currie; three seamen; and two passengers, one being young Angeline Publicover who was going to Halifax to buy her wedding dress.

All day in a light breeze the schooner sailed toward her destination and shortly after midnight Sambro Light, guardian of Halifax Harbour, was in sight. Then, without warning, a storm beat down. Entrance into Halifax was impossible and the little schooner was turned about to run back to LaHave. In the process the foresail split and the one can of kerosene on board upset. There would be no more light for passengers or crew. As the *Industry* neared LaHave the gale shifted again and drove the vessel out into the Atlantic. For three days and nights the vessel ran under bare poles. Somehow the crew managed to jettison the deck load of cord wood from the wildly pitching schooner but a water tank was struck and smashed. Only two gallons of fresh water remained. Salt water seeped into the provisions and for two weeks those on board sustained life on ten hard tack biscuits. The pounding of the seas started the seams and the vessel began to leak. Constant pumping was necessary to stay afloat.

Christmas dinner consisted of one soggy, raw potato found in the bilge and cut into seven pieces. Finally the exhausted crew could no longer man the pumps. On December 29, just when hope was gone, the stricken schooner was sighted by the barque *Providence*. Captain Coalfleet brought his vessel alongside and managed to pull the weakened complement of the *Industry* on board his own vessel. Less than an hour later the schooner went to the bottom. The rescued were taken to London and then returned to Halifax where they arrived on February 12, 1869, sixty-three days after they had left the LaHave River for the short sail to the capital city.

Now, in the first days of 1881, in command of the barque *Happy Home*, Captain Coalfleet was about to face his own time of disaster. On January 3 the *Happy Home* was nearing Saint John from Hamburg when in a blinding blizzard she struck the dreaded Trinity Ledge off Yarmouth, N.S. Held fast for two hours the barque then floated off half full of water and fell over on her beam ends. Mrs. Coalfleet and their eight-year-old daughter were lashed to the mizzen stays, the freezing seas constantly breaking over them. The crew of twelve, mostly Scandinavians, were also lashed to the stays while the mates endeavoured to keep ice from forming over the Coalfleet women.

All night long the helpless wreck drifted while Hiram Coalfleet tried to keep hope alive in the hearts of his family and crew, his own legs frozen to the knees. At the first light of dawn, just as the *Happy Home* was seen from shore and boats were putting off, Mrs. Coalfleet and her daughter died, clasped in each other's arms. The captain and crew were rescued while the misnamed *Happy Home* drifted ashore and went to pieces.

Hiram Coalfleet survived his ordeal but he was never the same man. Eight years later, in 1889, Emily Spicer wrote George while she was visiting friends in Hantsport, 'I am going to Captain Coalfleet's for supper tomorrow. He is a wreck of a man all used up with rheumatism. He never got over the chilling he got when his wife and daughter were frozen.'

1
Derelicts and
a Captain's Trial

A t the beginning of 1882 the *E.J. Spicer* was in Liverpool, England loading 1,396 tons of salt for New York. The ship sailed on January 27 and the passage was routine until March 1 when, nearing New York, a derelict was sighted. Captain Spicer wrote:

> This day a light breeze N.E. to S.E. with fine weather all day. All sail set. Ship going 4 to 9 knots. In company with a barque bound west and was gaining on her until 6 a.m. Seen a wreck to windward which proved to be the *Premier* of Yarmouth, N.S. abandoned and laying under a storm trysail. We ran alongside and hove to. Sent a boat and four men on board. Got some things, a mainsail, three old sails, some rope, 4½ barrels of flour and two cases of gin. Did not leave the wreck until 2 p.m. then made sail after setting her on fire. She was burning well the last we seen of her.

The derelict was the brigantine *Premier* of Yarmouth, N.S., 293 tons, built at Wedgeport, N.S. in 1872. She was reported abandoned on February 22, 1882 in Latitude 40°26'N. and Longitude 66°21'W. When found by the *E.J. Spicer* she was in Latitude 40°09'N. and Longitude 67°00'W.

The sighting of derelicts was not uncommon in the days of sail and George Spicer encountered several during his seagoing career. Occasionally vessels would continue to sail on after being abandoned. The *Rock Terrace*, a large Saint John ship, was sailing towards Hiogo, Japan in 1888 when she grounded on a coral reef during squally weather. The ship was leaking badly so that the pumps had to be manned constantly while the captain held on for Guam. After a month the island was reached but since the crew was exhausted from the continuous pumping and no assistance was available, the ship was abandoned and her complement rowed to Guam. The *Rock Terrace* sailed herself another 840 miles before running aground on Tarawa Island.

Many years later the four-masted schooner *Governor Parr*, built in Parrsboro, N.S., had an even longer, lonely voyage. In September 1923 the schooner sailed from Ingramport, N.S. for Buenos Aires with lumber. Soon after sailing, the vessel encountered heavy weather and suffered extensive damage. The crew was taken off by an American steamer but the schooner sailed on. The last time the *Governor Parr* was sighted, still afloat, was on October 24, 1924. Her position off the Canary Islands was some 2,000 miles east of where she had been abandoned.

In the years between 1887 and 1891 the American Hydrographic Service reported the sighting of 957 derelicts in one area alone off the Atlantic seaboard.

After leaving the wreck of the *Premier*, the *E.J. Spicer* continued her passage and reached New York three days later. Spicer had barely time to enter his vessel when he was summoned to sit on another Court of Inquiry. This inquiry concerned the loss of the Nova Scotia built barque *W.J. Stairs* and the proceedings were extensively described in a New York newspaper:

> The Naval Court of Inquiry appointed by the British Consul to investigate the loss of the bark *W.J. Stairs*, which was wrecked off Long Branch last Wednesday night, made known the result of their labors this morning. It will be remembered that Captain McKenzie, of the *Stairs*, charged that two pilot

boats had run away from his vessel, and the loss of the latter was indirectly attributed to this fact. The following is the finding of the court: —

The bark *W.J. Stairs* was built at Maitland, Nova Scotia, in 1870, of 1,088 tons register. She sailed from Liverpool on the 11th of last January with a cargo consisting of 1,200 tons of salt and a crew of fifteen men. Her cargo appears to have been properly stowed and the vessel in good condition and sufficiently manned. During the voyage, which was a rough one, nothing worthy of special mention occurred except the loss of a seaman named Charles Wilmer, who accidently fell from aloft into the sea on the 9th of February and was drowned. On the afternoon of the 1st of March the vessel was approaching the United States coast and was supposed by the master to be off the Long Island shore. During the afternoon a fog, with showers of rain, prevailed and the state of the atmosphere was such as to render it impossible to distinguish objects at any considerable distance. We believe that it was such as might have easily misled those on board the bark as to their own capability in this respect. No lights or landmarks were visible from the vessel previous to the stranding. The lights on board were in good order and burning at the time. At about half-past nine p.m. the bark went ashore on the New Jersey coast, in the neighborhood of Long Branch, and soon afterward broke up, the master and crew (with the exception of a lad named Joseph Dixon, who was washed overboard and drowned) being rescued with much difficulty in a breeches buoy sent from the life saving station on shore. Several shots were fired and lines carried away before communications could be established with the wreck, and the men subsequently saved no doubt owe their escape to the determination and perseverance of those employed at the Life Saving Station.

We are of opinion that the master would have shown greater prudence if, when at six o'clock he found himself approaching shallow water, he had hauled the ship to the wind and kept away from the coast, and that, in this respect, a lack of due judgment was displayed. The master, however, did not seem to have been aware of the existence of the prevailing current, which was setting westward, and which would no doubt in itself help to carry the ship closer to the New Jersey coast than could otherwise have been expected. There is a sufficient similarity between the soundings in this neighborhood and those on the coast of Long Island, to have misled the master as to his position.

While we are not of opinion, that any error in judgment on the part of those employed in the navigation of the bark was sufficiently gross to require us to deal with the certificate of any person on board, we consider it our duty to censure Kenneth McKenzie, master of the bark *W.J. Stairs*, and he is hereby censured and warned of the necessity of exercising greater caution hereafter when approaching the coast in this neighborhood, in thick weather.

J. PIERREPONT EDWARDS, H.B.M. Consul, Pres't,
HORATIO McKAY, Master, steamship *Parthia*,
GEO. D. SPICER, Master, ship *E.J. Spicer*,
New York, March 8, 1882.

8
Murder of the Mate

*F*ollowing the Court of Inquiry into the loss of the *W.J. Stairs*, George Spicer took his ship to London with a cargo of oil and brought her back to New York with chalk, baled rags and paper.

On August 4, 1882 the *E.J. Spicer* was nearly ready to sail again when the newly-married mate, Daniel Spicer, was murdered. Captain Spicer's first notation was:

> At 8:30 a.m. the tug came with four men and towed the ship off the Battery where we anchored. I left the ship at 10 a.m. in the tug boat. The shipping master sent off some of the men as they were shipped. At 11 a.m. one of them stabbed and killed the mate, Daniel Spicer, instantly. O My God to be sent to Eternity by such a fellow. Got the body on shore to the morgue at 5 p.m.

On August 7 the *E.J. Spicer* sailed for London with a cargo of refined oil and a new mate. On arrival George wrote his sister Antoinette and elaborated further on the murder:

> We are here after a good run of 22 days from the Gull but I have sad news to tell you. On the 4th of August poor Dan was stabbed to the heart by a sailor without provocation and died instantly. It was a

shocking murder and I will try to tell you about it.

The tug and crew were ordered for 8 a.m. Men were scarce so only four were brought on board. We towed off the Battery and anchored. At 10 a.m. I went on shore in the tug boat. Then at 11 a.m. there were two men sent on board. They went to the forecastle to change their clothes and was a long time. The 2nd mate went to tell them to come out and they had a good deal to say so he left them and the mate went soon after and said, 'It is time you were out,' and after awhile they came out and one of them used a knife on Dan. The second mate had gone for a tackle and turned and saw Dan try to take a capstan bar from the man when he drew a knife and drove it into Dan who fell dead. There was some of the men seizing off some of the head stays and they did not hear anything, it was done so quickly. The knife cut three ribs and went through Dan's heart. They locked the fellow up and the carpenter came for me. As soon as I saw him (carpenter) I knew there was trouble but I did not expect anything so awful. It has aged me I can tell you.

The account in a New York newspaper casts a somewhat different light on the affair:

Coroner Brady this afternoon began the inquest in the case of Daniel Spicer, mate of the British ship *E.J. Spicer*, who was stabbed and killed yesterday off Ellis' Island by Patrick O'Carew, a seaman. Edward Fish, the cabin boy of the ship, testified as follows: — "We were about to sail yesterday; the mate came aboard and gave some orders about the tackle; I heard the mate tell the prisoner to go and fetch the tackle; he (the prisoner) turned around and said, 'Call me by my name, Paddy;' the mate then kicked him once; the prisoner then ran and picked up a capstan bar; the mate then seized it and a scuffle ensued in which the mate got the bar and then took Paddy by the neck; Paddy then pulled out his knife and stabbed the mate in the left breast; the mate fell on the deck; the prisoner was at once placed under arrest and locked up by the carpenter; after the mate fell Paddy said, 'I knew him before today; I know all about him.' "

Oscar B. Morris, the second mate of the ship, testified that the deceased, after having been started, raised the capstan bar which he had taken from the prisoner, as if to strike him when the prisoner cried with an oath, "I'll cut you all to pieces."

Alfred Ramsden, a seaman, corroborated the foregoing testimony. The jury rendered a verdict against the accused and he was committed to the Tombs to await the action of the Grand Jury.

The mate was recently married and his young wife had come on here (from Spencers Island) to bid him goodby, little knowing it was to be their last parting in this world.

A letter from a friend later advised Captain Spicer that due to a lack of evidence, Patrick O'Carew received only a two-year prison term.

If George Spicer portrays an obvious bias on the side of the mate, who was his cousin, the newspaper story tends to picture Daniel Spicer in the mold of the old-time bucko mate handy with fist and boot. The truth probably lies somewhere in between. Daniel Spicer was well-liked and respected by those who knew him. Yet officers of the nineteenth century sailing vessels had to demand discipline; lives could depend on it; and if physical force was necessary, they did not hesitate to use it. It is worthy of note that author Frederick William Wallace who was well acquainted with many officers and seamen who sailed on these old windships made the flat statement, 'No sailor who behaved himself, obeyed orders and knew his work was ever abused or ill-treated aboard a Bluenose ship.'

9

Sailing to the Far East and a Hurricane

*T*here was a distinct pattern to the voyages of Captain George D. Spicer over the more than four decades he commanded sailing vessels. For the first twenty years he was on the North Atlantic run, principally from New York to such ports as London, Liverpool, Rotterdam, Antwerp, Havre and Bordeaux, with occasional side passages to Montreal and Cuba. Then, in 1888, he sailed to Shanghai and, for the next several years, most of his voyages would take him to the Far East and to ports on the west coasts of North and South America. His final years at sea were devoted to passages to South America and to destinations in the Caribbean and the Gulf of Mexico. It was a pattern dictated by one fact alone, where the best freights were offering or, in the later years, where the only freights were offering.

In 1885 Spicer left the *E.J. Spicer* and took command of the ship *Charles S. Whitney* launched at Spencers Island on July 14. A large ship of 1,651 tons and named after a member of the J.F. Whitney Company, the vessel would be Spicer's home for the next six years. He continued his passages across the North Atlantic until 1888 when, on one arrival in New York, he learned that the Whitney had been chartered to Shanghai with refined oil:

> I did not feel pleased about it at all but there is no help for it. It is a good charter.

The *Charles S. Whitney* sailed from New York for Shanghai on July 3, 1888. Captain Spicer had with him Emily Jane, their six-year-old son Stanley, and twenty officers and men. The path the ship would sail down through the South Atlantic, around the Cape of Good Hope and across the Indian Ocean did not follow the old adage that 'the shortest distance between two points is a straight line.' Instead of sailing on a generally southeasterly course from New York directly to the Cape of Good Hope then close around the cape and on acoss the Indian Ocean, the *Whitney* would follow a much longer course. On leaving New York Spicer would take the ship on a long, shallow loop to near mid-ocean then head southerly, crossing the Line in Longitude 27°55'W., passing Cape de Sao Roque on the easterly bulge of South America. He would continue south until reaching Latitude 32°S before beginning a gradual swing to the eastward, crossing the Indian Ocean in close to Latitude 40°S.

This was not a route of Captain Spicer's invention. He was following the recommendation of a great American oceanographer and wind expert, Matthew Fontaine Maury. Before Maury, whose life encompassed the years 1806 to 1873, vessels sailing to Australia from North Atlantic ports did follow a more or less straight line, keeping as far to the eastward of Cape de Sao Roque as possible, passing close to the Cape of Good Hope and sailing eastward across the Indian Ocean in much higher latitudes. Then a voyage of 120 days to Australia was considered good.

Maury advised Australian-bound vessels to cross the Line near Longitude 30°W. and then, run down through the southeast trades until they picked up the steady westerlies, before proceeding to the eastward in about Latitude 45°S., or even further south if ice and weather conditions permitted. He cautioned that the season of the year and the state of the ship would dictate how far to the south a ship should venture. The old clippers, in following his suggested route, were able to shorten the voyage to Australia by more than forty days.

In addition to Maury, there was another man to whom all navigators of Spicer's time owed a debt of gratitude. He was Captain James Cook, the eighteenth century British Naval officer, who induced a clockmaker friend, John Harrison, to develop a reliable sea-going clock for mariners. Prior to this time the greatest enemies of clocks at sea were the movements of vessels and the variations of temperatures between the tropics and cold northerly waters. Harrison's solution was a meld of various metals which together compensated for the stresses of movement and of heat and cold. Thus an accurate chronometer was born for the benefit of navigators the world over. It is also to Captain Cook that credit is accorded for the means to prevent scurvy among crews undertaking long voyages. In consultation with far-thinking naval surgeons, Cook discovered that a constant supply of fresh fruit and vegetables would successfully combat the dreaded disease. Captain James Cook was killed by natives on Hawaii in 1779 but his contributions to seafarers lived on.

In late August 1888 the *Charles S. Whitney* was west of the Cape of Good Hope in Latitude 40^{0}S. On track to Shanghai the ship was 'running her easting down' and George Spicer described something of the weather conditions in these lower latitudes:

August 27 — Gale increasing. Ship burying herself in water. Decks full. Took in foresail and topsail. Hove ship to under lower fore and main topsails for 18 hours. Ship making bad weather a great part of the time. I have never seen so much water on deck in any vessel before.

August 28 — This day a hard gale S.W. to W.S.W. attended with violent squalls of rain, hail and snow. A very high sea running. Decks full of water and everything washed from its place. Forecastle and all parts of the forward house full of water by times and plenty of water in some parts of the after cabin, everyway a bad day and nobody slept much.

When she was at sea Emily kept her own diary and her record for this passage remains. The detail of her entries for the same two days provides a graphic description of conditions aboard the *Whitney*:

August 27 — This day a whole gale to a hurricane. At 2 a.m. the wind went from N.W. to S.W. in a squall and blowed hard. At 4 a.m. took in the foresail and lower mizzen topsail. 9 a.m. wind more moderate and looking much finer and barometer raising slowly. Set the foresail and lower mizzen topsail. At noon gale increasing and ship rolling to leeward and filling its decks with water. Took in foresail and mizzen topsail and hove the ship to. At 2 p.m. wind blowing a hurricane and decks full of water and washing things to pieces. Spare spars went to leeward but got them secured without any damage. A very heavy sea running and violent squalls of hail and snow. A good deal of water in the cabin. The poor sailors had a hard time. Quantities of water in their apartment and some of their clothes washed out of the forecastle. The galley and carpenter's shop also had a great quantity of water in them but the steward managed to get us our meals alright. Stanley thought it fun to be sliding with the roll of the ship but when night come he got scairt and would not sleep in his bed. I don't think I ever saw a worse gale of wind and never anything like the amount of water on deck. Distance 100 miles.

August 28 — This day commences with a hard gale S.W. to W.S.W. attended with violent squalls of rain, hail and snow and a very high sea running. Decks full of water by times. Forecastle and any place forward has a great deal of water in them and a good deal of water in some parts of our cabin. No one slept much last night. I guess the poor sailors had no dry place to sleep or any dry clothes to put on. 7 a.m. squared away and run E.N.E. Was hove to for eighteen hours. 11 a.m. set foresail and mizzen topsail. 4 p.m. gale moderated some. Set upper main topsail. 8 p.m. set fore topsail. Squalls still very heavy. There has been no regularity about the sea. It seems to be every which way and would come over the ship from all parts. I have heard of gales off the Cape of Good Hope and have experienced one but do not wish another. Stanley and I have been close persons for two days. The poor hens and pigs (housed in pens on deck) have had a hard time of it. The hen coop come pretty near washing over. If it had it would have been good-bye hens. Distance 80 miles.

This was the weather the *Charles S. Whitney* experienced as she sailed ever eastward in Latitude 40⁰S. On September 13 Captain Spicer noted that it had been four weeks since they had last sighted a vessel. It would be another thirty days before one came in sight. The South Indian Ocean was a lonely expanse of water at times, much different than the more heavily travelled North Atlantic.

The *Whitney* sailed on until November 28 when a pilot came on board and the passage of 148 days was nearly over. It was by no means a record time but Captain Spicer noted that one vessel that left New York some five weeks before them and another that left three weeks before them had not arrived. Emily's closing note on the voyage was:

Sunday, December 2, 1888 — 7 a.m. the tug took hold and towed us part way where we had to stop and lighten some cargo before going up to Shanghai. George went up in the tugboat, telegraphed home and got our letters. A good lot of them for which I am very thankful. George got on board at 6 p.m. and I read letters from that time until about nine when my eyes got too sore so stopped until morning. I am truly thankful that our dear ones (at home) are all well.

The brigantine **Amazon,** later the mystery vessel **Mary Celeste.**

Courtesy New Brunswick Museum

The brig **Globe,** 289 tons, George Spicer's first command.

The barque **J.F. Whitney,** 701 tons, built Spencers Island, 1872.

The ship **E.J. Spicer,** 1317 tons, built at Spencers Island, 1880.

The ship **Charles S. Whitney,** 1651 tons, launched at Spencers Island in July, 1885.

The ship **Glooscap,** 1734 tons, launched Spencers Island, 1891. Shown in Tacoma, 1901.   *Courtesy Conrad Byers*

Part of **Glooscap's** crew. Captain Spicer standing centre of back row with felt hat. In front is his stepson, Ingram Banks. Circa 1901.

Courtesy Conrad Byers

George D. and Emily Jane Spicer.

The barquentine **Perfection,** 509 tons. Last square-rigger built at Spencers Island. Launched 1893. Destroyed by fire, North Atlantic, August 1896.

Courtesy Mrs. Emily Currie

Some investors in Spencers Island shipbuilding. *Back row from left:* Johnson Spicer, Capt. George D. Spicer, N.W. Eaton. *Front:* W.H. Bigelow, Antoinette (Spicer) Williams, Amasa Loomer.

The Spencers Island Shipyard. Schooner **Myrtle Leaf** on the stocks.

Courtesy Conrad Byers

A typical three-masted or tern schooner under sail with deck load.

Courtesy Conrad Byers

10
Launching of the Glooscap

*G*eorge Spicer brought the *Charles S. Whitney* back to new York via the Philippines with a cargo of sugar and hemp, arriving on June 16, 1889, seventeen days short of a year since their departure. There followed a round voyage to London and then the *Whitney* was again chartered to Shanghai with refined oil. This time Spicer took Emily Jane and their fifteen-year-old daughter Gertrude. Departing New York on November 20, 1889 the ship reached Shanghai on April 23, 1890 after a voyage of 20,730 miles via the Cape of Good Hope. The return voyage by way of Hong Kong with a mixed cargo of wool, straw braid and chinaware was uneventful and the ship arrived in New York on January 12, 1891. It was Spicer's last voyage on the *Charles S. Whitney*.

Back home at Spencers Island the new ship *Glooscap* was on the stocks and at 1,734 gross tons she would be the largest ship ever built in Spencers Island or, indeed, in Cumberland County. On her, Captain Spicer would finish out his seafaring career.

As was his wont, George Spicer was busy helping to finish the new ship and he was corresponding almost daily with the J.F. Whitney Company regarding charters for the various Spencers Island vessels. On August 5, 1891 the *Glooscap* was launched and a newspaper of the day gave a lively portrayal of the event:

Last Wednesday was emphatically a gala day at Spencers Island. The weather was fine — ideally fine — and at an early hour the country side was alive with travellers all bent on seeing the "$75,000 slide." About sunrise schooner *Amy D.* which had just arrived with a party of excursionists hoisted her colors and a little later the spars of the big ship became gay with bunting. The four-masted schooner *Uruguay* next showed her colors and flags were soon waving from nearly every vessel in the Bay and from several buildings in the village. As the day grew older the influx of visitors increased and there was something very much like a procession on every road leading to the village while the dooryards for a mile on either side were crowded with carriages. The big ship was of course the centre of attraction and her decks were thronged all the while with a constantly changing stream of visitors. It was noticed that Cumberland's largest ship had been appropriately named *Glooscap* after the legendary hero of the Micmacs who, if reports are true, was in the habit of indulging in high jinks along the shore. The spot where the big ship was built was apparently his favorite picnic ground and it is stated that on one occasion, when annoyed by the tax collector or the newspaper reporter, or something, he overturned his kettle in the Bay. That part of the story is not doubted by anyone who has ever visited the place, for the kettle may be seen at this day and is called Spencers Island.

All the morning arrivals continued by land and sea and the refreshment tables and dining booths were soon doing a brisk business. Mr. Johnson Reid, of Parrsboro had an improvised photograph gallery on the grounds and had no lack of patrons. The revolving swings did a roaring trade and made a horrible creaking, and the persuasive faker was on hand seeking whom he might devour.

As the tide approached high water mark, everybody's attention seemed to concentrate on the ship. The last blocks were split out, and at about 12:50 the slide commenced. The launch was one of the prettiest ever seen. The ship which represents so much labor and capital, so much care and skill, and so many bright anticipations, glided majestically into the Bay, bowed politely to the crowd on shore and swept outward in a long graceful curve toward the overturned kettle. A schooner from Hall's Harbor with her decks thronged with visitors, arrived just after the launch was over and another, equally crowded, arrived from Margaretsville a few minutes later.

Among the shareholders in the new vessel was the Honourable Charles Tupper who, in 1896, would briefly become the Prime Minister of Canada. Tupper was an investor in several of the Spencers Island vessels and a long-time correspondent with Spicer.

Shortly after the launch of the *Glooscap*, the ship *Savona*, fresh from the yard of W.P. Cameron in South Maitland, N.S., anchored off Spencers Island and her captain, George Stailing, and his wife came ashore and had dinner with George and Emily Spicer. In years hence the *Savona* and Captain Stailing would each be the focus of tragic news.

11
Loss of Two Captains

George Stailing, a native of Annapolis Royal, N.S., was a veteran master mariner who would remain with the *Savona* for several years after her 1891 launching. Then, in January 1899 he was master of the four-masted British barque *Andelana*. The *Andelana* had sailed into Tacoma harbour, discharged her cargo and was at anchor. As the vessel was riding empty of cargo, she was supported by large log booms on either side of her, chained to the hull. One evening the barque simply disappeared. At dusk she had been seen riding to her anchor, the next morning there was no sign of her. Dragging efforts and the work of an intrepid diver established that the vessel had gone down in the night. It was assumed that a squall hit the barque and she had capsized. Whatever the reason, the *Andelana* took Captain Stailing and fourteen of her complement to a watery grave.

For her part, the *Savona* was a fine ship of over 1,600 registered tons. In March 1901 the ship departed Sydney, Australia for Rotterdam with a cargo of oil shale. Her master was Captain Hedley MacDougall who had his wife with him. The ship crossed the Pacific, rounded Cape Horn and was off the Falkland Islands when, one morning, the sea began to make up and a squall carried away the fore topmast. The crew was busy clearing away the wreckage and Captain MacDougall was on top of the after cabin supervising the work when the ship was pooped by a giant wave. The force of the wave wrecked the after part of the vessel, killed the two men at the wheel and destroyed the ship's binnacle and steering apparatus. The after cabin was swept clean, tearing out both ends but leaving the sides and cabin top intact. Mrs. MacDougall, below in her berth, was swept along in the deluge of water to the foot of the mizzen mast but miraculously escaped with only a bruise. The battered body of the dead steward lay beside her.

There was not a sign of Captain MacDougall and it was assumed he had been washed overboard. The resourceful mate took charge, rigged a temporary steering gear, made emergency repairs and twenty-six days later the *Savona* limped into Montevideo. Captain MacDougall had a pet cat on board and several days after the accident the cat began to act strangely as if trying to attract attention. Finally, on the eighth day after the vessel was pooped, some of the crew followed the cat to a pile of wreckage still on the forward deck. Underneath they found the body of Captain MacDougall, his arms folded just as they had been when he was last seen standing on top of the after cabin. There was no sign of injury, just a tiny blue mark on his temple.

12

The Death of Emily Jane

*T*he *Glooscap*'s maiden voyage took her from Spencers Island to Liverpool, England with lumber. From there she towed to Cardiff and loaded coal for Cape Town, South Africa where she arrived on February 11, 1892. There were no cargoes offering in Cape Town so Captain Spicer took the ship in ballast across the Indian Ocean to Taltal on the Chilean coast. Here he was able to take on a cargo of nitrate and after a passage of seventy-four days, by way of Cape Horn, arrived in New York on September 5. In a year less ten days the *Glooscap* had circumnavigated the world. Bad news awaited George Spicer and it concerned his wife.

Emily.Jane had not been well in recent years. On their last voyage to Shanghai she frequently complained of feeling tired. George had taken her to doctors at home and in New York but the physicians could not, or would not, give him much in the way of a definite diagnosis.

Now he found his wife in Boston critically ill with cancer. He went to her as soon as the *Glooscap* was moored in New York and was shocked by her appearance and condition: 'She looks so changed from what she was, so much thinner.' For the next few weeks he commuted between Boston and the ship in New York and consulted doctors in both cities but received no encouragement. Emily wanted to go home so George turned the *Glooscap* over to his brother Edmund and on October 19:

I carried my dear Emily down to the carriage and got her on the steamer for Saint John. She was very tired but otherwise was much the same. My sister Nettie and I stayed with her all night in the stateroom.

The next day in Saint John they transferred to a small coastal steamer for the run home. Emily was very weak and for the next few days she drifted in and out of consciousness. In one of her more lucid moments she asked her husband to promise not to ship either of their two younger sons as sailors. It was a promise George Spicer made and one he lived to regret. Then on October 29, 1892:

At 1 a.m. my poor dear wife passed away. She did not suffer so very much that we could tell. We passed a very sad day. Several friends and relatives were in during the evening.

The final chapter was written two days later, on October 31:

A little before 4 p.m. we reached the grave and laid away in the cold earth all that remained of the one I loved so fondly. My heart was fit to break.

Emily Jane was just a few weeks short of her forty-fourth birthday at the time of her death.

The marriage of Emily and George Spicer had been a love affair from the time they married in 1868 until the end. Although he would remarry a few years later, Emily was always first and until his own death many years later, George noted each and every anniversary of their marriage and her death in his diary. There were those who remembered him as an old man saying to himself as he worked about his yard, 'My poor dear Emily,' over and over again. It was something his second wife understood and accepted.

George remained home for two months then went to New York. The *Glooscap* was chartered to Melbourne with oil and general cargo and George threw himself into preparations for the voyage. Life had to go on.

13

To Australia and Strife on the Glooscap

*I*n sailing to Australia Captain Spicer would be following a path well travelled by the clipper ships of a few decades earlier. The discovery of gold in Australia in 1851 sparked tremendous marine traffic to that country almost immediately. In 1852, 102,000 people arrived in the colony of Victoria and within eighteen months the population of Melbourne rose from 23,000 to 70,000. In the five years between 1852 and 1857, when the gold rush was at its height, 100,000 Englishmen, 60,000 Irish, 50,000 Scots, 4,000 Welsh, 8,000 Germans, 1,500 French, 3,000 Americans and 25,000 Chinese were among those who arrived on Australian shores to seek their fortunes.

This rush to get to the gold fields created a fierce demand for fast ships, far beyond the abilities of the traditional British shipyards to cope; and yards in Maine and New Brunswick in particular were quick to help fill the void. New Brunswick contributed several clippers, the best known coming out of Saint John, the *Marco Polo*, and she made her reputation on her first voyage Down Under. In 1852 when the *Marco Polo* was about to sail from Liverpool to Melbourne her master, Captain James 'Bully' Forbes, boasted he would have the ship back in Liverpool within six months. People laughed but he went out in sixty-eight days and came back in seventy-six. The round voyage, including the time in Melbourne, consumed just five months and twenty-one days.

It was this era that made a Nova Scotian-born designer and builder, Donald MacKay, world-famous. He had moved to Boston at a young age and it was there he designed and built clippers like the *Lightning, Sovereign of the Seas, Flying Cloud,* and *Champion of the Seas,* ships that will be remembered as long as sailing ships are remembered.

These clippers were built for speed, carrying immense clouds of canvas and large crews to work them. The clipper *Lightning,* for example, measured 1,468 registered tons and spread 13,000 yards of canvas. Captain Spicer's *Charles S. Whitney* measured 1,651 registered tons but only spread 7,079 yards of canvas. The clippers could regularly record speeds of sixteen to eighteen knots and better while George Spicer's cargo carriers rarely exceeded twelve. If the *Lightning* could log over 400 miles in twenty-four hours, none of Spicer's vessels ever exceeded 300. They were different vessels built for different purposes.

When the *Glooscap* departed New York for Melbourne on March 13, 1893 she would follow in the tracks of the old clipper ships. The ship was only six days out when Captain Spicer lost the third sailor of his career:

> At 10:45 a.m. called the watch to take in sail. Alex. McLean got up (on deck) alright but broke a blood vessel and was dead in fifteen minutes.

This brief entry was followed by a second on the next day:

> At 8 a.m. we buried Alex. McLean, A.B., 48 years old who hailed from Inverness, Scotland. It was a solemn sight to see all the crew standing around in the rain bare-headed while I read the burial service and give a short address before we slid his body overboard. The weather was bad and I felt very sad myself. It brought to mind the sad loss of my dear wife.

The *Glooscap* crossed the Line on April 6 and on May 4 passed close to the island of Tristan da Cunha in the mid South Atlantic. Spicer worked the ship down to about Latitude 39⁰S.

before running east. The *Glooscap* arrived in Melbourne on June 18 after a passage of ninety-seven days in which she logged 14,813 miles.

The cook and stewardess on the *Glooscap*, a husband and wife team, had caused George Spicer no end of trouble on the passage to Australia by their constant fighting. When the ship reached port matters became a little more serious when, in one confrontation, the stewardess stabbed her husband in the shoulder and hip. The wounds did not require his hospitalization but the cook was laid up for a time and unable to work. A few days later the couple resumed their private war and this time the cook had his wife arrested. A Melbourne newspaper brought the tale of marital strife on shipboard to public attention:

OTHELLO AND DESDEMONA
"THEIR LIFE ON THE OCEAN WAVE"

A young woman named Alice Bobb was charged at the South Melbourne Court this forenoon with wounding her husband, William Bobb.

Sub-inspector Swale prosecuted and Mr. Daly appeared for the accused.

Prosecutor, a colored man, deposed that he was steward on board the American ship *Glooscap*, berthed at the south wharf, and his wife was the stewardess. Last Saturday morning witness was in the galley when accused came in and asked for hot water. He told her the water had been taken aft to the cabin when she abused him. He answered her in similar language, when she snatched up a knife and stabbed him in the shoulder and above the right hip. He ran aft, and his wife ran after him flourishing the knife and calling out she would murder him. The captain dressed his wounds and yesterday he had to go to a doctor.

To Mr. Daly: He was married to accused a little over six months. They had a quarrel during the voyage from New York and he slapped his wife's face.

Mr. Daly argued that accused was justified in acting as she had in self-defense. He had assaulted her on several occasions and tried to choke her when the knife was used. He called Accused, who said she was married to prosecutor in New York. Shortly after the marriage and previous to the sailing of the vessel her husband gave her a couple of black eyes and on the voyage he assaulted her, and she was doctored by the captain. On the Sunday morning when she went into the galley for the water prosecutor called her vile names, caught her by the throat and as he had a steel and a knife in his hands she got excited, caught up a knife and cut him. She did not chase him along the deck with the knife in her hand and say she would murder him.

Captain George Spicer stated that on the voyage from New York, Bobb and his wife had several squabbles, and on one occasion he struck her a severe blow behind the ear. After the row on Sunday last Mrs. Bobb said her husband caught her by the throat and tried to strangle her.

The charge was altered to one of common assault and accused was fined £5 or one month's imprisonment.

A disgusted Captain Spicer paid the fine but vowed it would come out of the Bobbs' wages. That night the couple went off to the theatre as happy as newlyweds.

14

Down Under and a Fire in Halifax

*T*he *Glooscap* departed Melbourne for London on September 2, 1893 with a cargo of wool, tallow and mixed goods. Sailing by way of Cape Horn, the ship reached London after a passage of ninety-nine days in which the ship logged 14,865 miles. It is worthy of note that the passage was just fifty-two miles and two days longer than the outward run from New York to Melbourne via the Cape of Good Hope.

From London the *Glooscap* carried cement to New York and was then chartered to Newcastle, Australia with a mixed cargo. She sailed on April 30, 1894 and arrived in Newcastle after a voyage of ninety-five days.

Almost as soon as the vessel docked some of the crew went on shore to celebrate. One was arrested for being drunk and disorderly and Captain Spicer decided to leave him in jail as he had been a troublemaker on the passage out. It was a subterfuge rather reminiscent of Captain James 'Bully' Forbes when he took the *Marco Polo* into Melbourne on her maiden voyage in 1852, swearing he would make the round voyage back to Liverpool in six months.

Once in Melbourne, Forbes was afraid his crew would desert and run off to the gold fields. Crews were impossible to find in the Australian port so as soon as his vessel was moored, Forbes had the entire gang jailed on a trumped-up charge of insubordination. There they languished until the *Marco Polo* was ready to sail. This action did not endear Forbes to his men but that did not unduly bother him. After all, when one of his ships was sailing through gales in southern latitudes, Captain Forbes reportedly stood on the after deck with a loaded revolver in each hand in case his terrified crew attempted to shorten sail. 'Bully' Forbes was a man who had truly earned his nickname.

Captain Forbes enjoyed a world-wide reputation as master of the clipper ships *Marco Polo* and *Lightning*. But when he wrecked another clipper, the *Schomberg*, he became a changed man, although absolved of any blame by a Court of Inquiry. By the early 1860s he was described as being seedy in appearance and somewhat down and out. Forbes died at the age of fifty-two in Liverpool and on his tombstone was carved his main claim to fame, 'Master of the Famous *Marco Polo*.'

In Newcastle, the *Glooscap* loaded coal for Manila and then went on to Ilo Ilo in the Philippines where she took on 2,900 tons of sugar for Halifax. On January 12, 1895 she sailed for the Nova Scotia port and arrived in the harbour after a passage of 107 days.

The *Glooscap* was docked at the Richmond wharf and part of her cargo discharged. On May 9 the vessel was moved across the harbour to Woodside to finish unloading and to take on a cargo of deals. It was a move which undoubtedly saved the vessel. The *Halifax Morning Chronicle* of May 21, 1895 tells the story:

> The long wharf with freight sheds and the coaling pier at Richmond were destroyed by fire yesterday morning. The (earlier) fire at the deep water terminus, when the elevator and wharves were destroyed, proved to be a heavy loss to Halifax from a commercial standpoint. The fire of yesterday morning will prove no less disastrous as the only coaling pier in the city has been swept away. 58 cattle were destroyed. The loss by the fire is estimated to be at least $150,000.

15

Mutiny on the Launberga

*G*eorge Spicer left the *Glooscap* in Halifax and returned home. He underwent an operation for the removal of a toe and following convalescence he was immersed in the business operations of the Spencers Island vessels. Then, about this time, Mrs. Janetta Banks entered the picture. When or how they met is not known but the circumstances were plain. She was a widow with a young family, he was now fifty and lonesome. It was a match advantageous to both and in March 1897 they were married.

When Spicer rejoined the *Glooscap* in the spring of 1897, she had been chartered from New York to Melbourne with oil. The ship sailed on April 21 and followed her usual path around the Cape of Good Hope. She arrived on July 30, discharged her cargo and sailed for Newcastle to load coal for Manila. In Newcastle Captain Spicer found thirteen vessels all loading coal for Manila. Several were Maritimers including three built at Maitland: the ship *Norwood*, barque *Calburga* and the barque *Launberga*.

Around every vessel there are stories. They may concern fast passages, rescues at sea, shipwreck, heroism, cowardice or innumerable other events. The *Launberga* had her own story. A large barque of over 1,200 tons, she had been launched in 1893 by Adams MacDougall in South Maitland. Two years later, in 1895, she was anchored at Ilo Ilo under the command of Captain John Curry MacDougall, a brother of her builder. The barque had been in Manila where the crew, for some reason, had not been allowed shore leave but they were promised such leave in Ilo Ilo. However, the British Vice-Consul in that port would not allow the crew to go on shore because of troubles with the crews of some earlier vessels. He placed two armed native policemen on the *Launberga* to enforce his directive. The crew of the barque was in an ugly mood.

When a bumboat, unknown to Captain MacDougall, brought liquor to his seamen, they got drunk which inflamed their anger even more. They decided to take matters into their own hands and rushed the mate who was an elderly man. The bo'sun joined the fray to help the mate who managed to struggle aft to the poop. Here six of the drunken sailors attacked him again.

It was now that Captain MacDougall, below in his cabin, heard the noise and rushed on deck. Sizing up the situation at a glance, he hurried below for his revolver and told his wife to stay there with their baby. MacDougall returned to the deck where the sailors rushed him. He fired one shot over their heads, unwilling yet to shoot a man but they attacked him with knives. One slashed the captain from the hairline to the middle of his cheek. He then shot one man and fought the sailors hand to hand while the blood poured over his face. The bo'sun ran in and placed himself between his wounded captain and the enraged sailors. Mrs. MacDougall, worried about her husband, came on deck and ran to his side. She was knocked down, kicked and trampled underfoot. The two policemen did nothing.

The mutineers were finally distracted by the cries of their dying comrade, the one shot by Captain MacDougall. There was a moment of indecision then they loaded him in a boat and rowed off for medical aid. They were only gone a short time when Captain Ned Hurlburt came on board. He had brought his vessel, the barque *Bowman B. Law*, to anchor nearby only an hour before and it was to his vessel the mutineers had rowed. Hurlburt was suspicious of their story and had come to the *Launberga* as quickly as he could. The police were summoned and the mutineers arrested. One died in prison and the others were sentenced to various terms of incarceration. The officers of the *Launberga* and Mrs. MacDougall all recovered from their ordeal but Captain MacDougall carried the scars of the encounter for the rest of his life.

George Spicer would meet once more with the *Launberga*. In 1904 when he was in New York, Spicer was asked to supervise some repairs to the ship for her owner and builder, Adams MacDougall. The *Launberga* eventually went under the Swedish flag and sailed until the early 1920s when she was dismantled.

16
The Spanish-American War

*T*he *Glooscap* delivered her coal in Manila then towed to Ilo Ilo where she loaded 2,850 tons of sugar for Philadelphia. The return voyage was routine and the ship arrived in Philadelphia after a passage of 109 days port to port. The ship was immediately chartered back to Manila with coal but this time there was a difference.

The Spanish-American War had broken out and the coal was destined for Commodore Dewey's American fleet in Manila. In world history the war was little more than a minor skirmish but, in the story of George D. Spicer, it deserves a little background.

The war had its beginnings in Cuba which, along with Puerto Rico, comprised nearly all that was left of Spain's once extensive empire in the New World. In 1895 a revolution had broken out as Cubans sought to overthrow their oppressive Spanish rulers. The Spaniards retaliated with brutal force, ordering much of the population into concentration camps where they died by the thousands. Even these atrocities might not have stirred much attention in the United States except that the two newspaper giants of the day, Hearst and Pulitzer, were waging a bitter circulation war. Each sent large contingents of reporters to Cuba and soon stories were coming back to American readers of massacres, rapes, the starvation of non-combatants and other indignities. According to military historians some of the stories were true, some were largely embellished and others were frankly the products of reporters' imaginations. Be that as it may, the American people were aroused but it was two other events which brought the United States into the conflict. One was a letter written by the Spanish Ambassador to Washington in which he called President McKinley 'a weak man and a bidder for the admiration of the people.' The letter fell into the wrong hands, became public knowledge and Americans were outraged. The second event occurred on February 15, 1898 when the U.S. battleship *Maine* was blown up in Havana Harbour and 260 lives were lost. The Spanish were blamed and cries for retribution were heard throughout the land.

War with Spain was declared in April and Commodore Dewey was instructed to take his far eastern fleet to attack the Philippines. Dewey's fleet at the time consisted of the cruisers *Olympia, Boston, Raleigh, Concord* and the gunboat *Petrel*. He left the China coast and steamed for Manila where the venerable Spanish fleet was stationed. The ensuing battle was a rout and the American fleet suffered the loss of only one man — a victim of heat stroke. George Dewey was immediately promoted to Admiral and became the first American hero of the war.

The Spanish army, however, still controlled Manila and it was not until August 13 that the city was surrendered. The natives had hailed Dewey's naval force as their deliverers from tyranny but soon discovered that American plans for a free Cuba did not extend to the Philippines. In 1899 they rebelled and fought the Americans from island to island until 1901 when the uprisings were quelled — but at a cost of 4,300 American lives.

On June 26, 1898 Captain Spicer sailed from Philadelphia, uncertain of what he would find on arrival in Manila. All went well on the voyage and on October 31 the *Glooscap* was sailing by the island of Ponapi, one of the Caroline Islands. Spicer described the scene:

> The Sailing Directions said to be careful as the natives were not to be trusted. Imagine our surprise when we saw two boats with 45 men in them. The

natives had clothes on and hair cut; they wanted Bibles and religious books and we were able to fit them out. I asked them about the change, they said the Salvation Army had been among them. They were very mannerly and spoke fairly good English. They had a lot of hats, they made them something like a Panama hat. They did not beg for anything. There were 850 people on that small island. I bought all their hats.

It was an interesting interlude and it came just two weeks before personal disaster struck George Spicer.

17
Loss of a Son

*B*efore the *Glooscap* sailed for Manila in June 1898, Captain George Spicer and his son Whitney had several serious discussions. Whitney was nearly eighteen, had finished at Acacia Villa School and, above everything else, wanted to go to sea. In short he wanted to sign on the *Glooscap* for the voyage to the Philippines. The father, ever mindful of his promise to Emily, resisted but in the end Whitney won the day. When the *Glooscap* sailed, Whitney was in the fo'c'sle, an ordinary seaman.

On November 14, 1898 the ship was north of Luzon, the northern island in the Philippines Group. George Spicer described the events:

> This day commenced with a fresh gale N.E. to west. By 11 a.m. it was developing into a typhoon. Hove the ship to at noon. At 4 p.m. Whitney went with three others to secure the jib when the ship went into a sea and they all went overboard. The other three was got on board by throwing ropes, etc. but Whitney poor fellow could not swim and sunk to raise no more. O God what a sight for me his unhappy father to stand and see him drowned and not be able to help him in any way. The ship drove off from him. Just to think him so young and healthy and good spirits to be taken that

way. It is too much to bear but we know we are in God's hands and must be resigned as his ways are not ours. But it nearly breaks my heart to think of it. May God have mercy on his poor soul.

The voyage of the *Glooscap* had to continue. Three days after Whitney's drowning his father wrote, 'I sold most of Whitney's clothes. Poor boy. Something to remind me of him all the time.' The selling of a lost seaman's clothes was a way of the sea and there was no room for sentiment. Then on November 20:

We arrived in Manila without any more mishaps, 147 days from Philadelphia. Two days later we were towed to Cavite where Admiral Dewey's fleet was and discharged the cargo of coal. I had the first bill of lading the Admiral ever receipted. I was offered $1000 for it but had to send it to Washington. There was a lot of letters for Whitney which was hard to take.

While the ship was in Manila, George wrote his sister Antoinette about Whitney's death:

I could be quite contented here if we had not had the sad misfortune to lose my dear boy overboard. It seems too hard altogether but God's ways are not ours. Still it is very hard for me to say everything is for the best. It must have been a great shock to you all at home as well as to us on board the ship.

When I see Captain Smith's son here around the vessel just about as Whitney would have been, I can't keep the tears back. Captain Smith in the ship *Wildwood* has a son 21. Left school a short time ago just about like Whitney and they could not get him to go into any business at home. He wanted to go with them to sea. Mrs. Smith is so scared that something might happen to her son, she will hardly let him out of her sight. You know that is not my style. I never thought of danger and where a young fellow can get hold with his hands, he is safe. But this fatal sea broke right on top of them on the boom where there is not even a good chance to hold on. Sometimes I think things are to be and whatever we do can't help it or make any difference.

In early January 1899 Captain Spicer received orders to proceed to Ilo Ilo to load sugar for Philadelphia. However, as he noted, 'We can't go there now on account of the unsettled state of affairs there.' It was nearly the end of January before the ship could anchor in Ilo Ilo. On arrival Spicer wrote:

> In Ilo Ilo we found four American warships and two or three transports with 2200 troops to take the town which they did on February 11. The first gun was fired at 10:45 a.m. The natives set the place on fire and some took to the country and some to the ships. We had 42 men on board for three days. They felt bad to see their property burning up. On February 12 two other captains and myself went on shore. Found a sad sight. So much of the town burned down, about three-quarters of the place. Found out there had been a lot of looting by the American troops and the Europeans are very much put out with the Americans the way things have been done.

Due to the war, it took a long time to load the *Glooscap* and it was March 28 before the ship sailed for Philadelphia. It was a voyage with a strange aftermath.

18
The Ghost Ship

A fter leaving Ilo Ilo, the *Glooscap* sailed through the Sunda Strait, into the Indian Ocean, around the Cape of Good Hope and on to Philadelphia where she arrived on August 2 after a passage of 127 days port to port. It was strictly a routine voyage — or was it?

Shortly after the vessel's arrival a long story appeared in a Philadelphia newspaper, a story which has been oft-repeated and as recently as a few years ago on one Nova Scotian newspaper:

> A strange tale of the sea was brought into home waters by the crew of the British ship *Glooscap* from far-away Ilo Ilo in the Philippines. No more weird adventure is told in all annals of navigation than that which was an incident of her voyage through the loneliest part of the Indian Ocean. For many days on the homeward run, never to be forgotten by Captain George D. Spicer and his men, the *Glooscap* was accompanied on her way by a battered, almost shapeless hulk, a nameless derelict, which without sail and without steam hung persistently in her wake. The mystery of her occurrence was appalling to the crew of this good ship. With it were incidents which go to make up a true tale, stranger than the wildest dreams of the novelist of the sea.

The *Glooscap*, heavily laden with sugar for Philadelphia, weighed anchor from Ilo Ilo on March 28. Her voyage was a long one and through the most unfrequented of the earth's oceans. Nevertheless the ship sailed fast and there was no reasonable supposition on the part of the crew or captain that the run would be an eventful one. Anjer was passed on April 23 and for twenty succeeding days nothing occurred of any special mention. No sails appeared to break the monotony of sea and sky. The *Glooscap*, logging ten knots, ploughed steadily over the dreary waste of waters. On May 14, at four o'clock in the morning, a drifting hulk was reported on the western horizon.

The day broke cold, misty and rainy with a leaden sky. No more cheerless scene could have heralded the advent of the derelict. Still on the same track the *Glooscap* steadily approached it. There is no more saddening incident which can occur in the life of a sailor than an accidental meeting with one of these grim reminders of a great and unsolved disaster. It is a silent appeal to their blunted, better natures, never lost in view of their perilous vocation.

The battered hulk, now abeam of the *Glooscap*, appeared to be that of a full-rigged ship. Her masts had gone by the board and she was partially waterlogged. The waves gurgled dismally through her deserted deck house and splashed heavily on her rotten boards. She was a melancholy and gloomy spectacle; an embodiment of death and suffering; of the passing of many hardy souls.

Captain Spicer scrutinized the wreck closely. There was absolutely no clue to her identity. The *Glooscap* continued on her way. Rain began falling and fog descended intensifying the gloom. The unexpected meeting had its effect on the crew. There were no songs in the forecastle that night. The sailors endeavored to sleep, to forget the sad spectacle which they had involuntarily witnessed. Captain Spicer was aroused the next morning at daybreak. A frightened group stood outside the cabin door. 'My God, Captain, the wreck. Look it is following us,' and the boatswain pointed his finger astern of the *Glooscap.* Sure enough, scarcely three miles in his wake Captain Spicer saw the ominous visitor of the previous day.

Scarcely believing his eyes, he computed the distance during the past twelve hours. A rough guess placed it at 120 miles. A fear seized the old mariner. 'It is nothing boys, only the effect of an uncharted ocean current which must exist here. We will lose her in a few hours.' Nevertheless the crew continued to stand in trembling silence. They gazed in nameless dread on the Nemesis which followed closely. A sharp northeast gale was blowing. At the request of his men the captain set all sail on the *Glooscap.* Toward ten o'clock the wind blew with frightful violence. Listed far off to starboard and under a cloud of canvas which bent her mighty spars like reeds, the ship tore through the foaming waves with race-horse speed.

Night came on again but it was a night of horror. The dread harbinger of death followed on relentlessly. Day succeeded day but the apparent position remained the same. The more sensible ones of the crew sought to delude themselves with the thought that they were victims of hallucinations; the remainder never turned their eyes astern. For a week the novel chase continued. Despair and desperation had by this time seized the wretched tars. The long, continued mental excitement at last had its effect. They were like demented beings and the officers feared they knew not what from their madness and terror.

May 21, when the affairs of the *Glooscap* had reached a climax, the derelict had disappeared. At noon, or eight bells, her motion was observed to be retarded, soon she appeared a mere speck on the horizon and then passed into oblivion.

Thus was described one of the most remarkable incidents in the long history of seafaring. But was it true? Captain Spicer's record of the voyage makes no mention of a derelict nor did he ever mention it in later years. During the days when the wreck was supposed to be following the *Glooscap*, Spicer does report the sighting of two vessels, one he thought to be the Maitland-built barque *Strathearn*.

The most logical explanation for the story was provided by then eleven-year-old Ingram Banks who had accompanied his mother and stepfather on the voyage. He always remembered the voyage well but remembered nothing of a derelict, something which surely would have left an indelible impression. He was always certain that, after a long period at sea, one of the more imaginative sailors was on shore celebrating and fell in with a reporter who was looking for a story. So he gave him a good one.

19

The End In Sight

*T*he decade of the '90s had been busy and eventful years for George Spicer. His voyages had taken him five times to Australia and the Far East; he had made ports in England, Wales, South Africa, Chile and Nova Scotia as well as Philadelphia, New York and Norfolk. His last and largest command, the *Glooscap*, had been launched and, on the personal side, he had lost his wife and son and had remarried. As the old century ended Spicer would be embarking on the final phase of his long seafaring career. And the early years of the new century would see the end of the square-rigged windships.

It was not a sudden decline, indeed the First World War would bring a brief revival when ships' bottoms were desperately needed. But for all intents and purposes the first decade of the twentieth century would see the end of the stately old windjammers. By now the building of new square-riggers had practically ceased and most of those still sailing were getting old.

There were several reasons for their demise, particularly vessels built in the Maritime provinces. The development of steam-powered vessels had been going on for many decades. As early as 1838 the paddle-wheeler *Sirius* had steamed from London to New York in eighteen days, ten hours. Only two years later Samuel Cunard's *Britannia* made the same passage in just ten days. This was a time that sailing vessels could not hope to match and steamers could do so on a regularly scheduled basis. As steam-powered vessels gradually improved in both structure and power, they not only obtained lower insurance premiums thus offering lower freight rates, they also attracted many of the better young seamen. Young men of the early 1900s who aspired to careers at sea increasingly looked to steam as the way of the future. Also, there was no going aloft in howling gales or standing a trick at the wheel on the open deck of steamers. Life was simply much easier on the steam-powered vessels.

And there were other reasons. The opening of the Suez Canal in 1869 gave steamships a tremendous advantage over sailing vessels which had to sail around the Cape of Good Hope. This forced many of the British iron sailing ships out of their far eastern trades and into direct competition with Maritimers who were carrying oil from the United States to Britain and Europe as well as nitrates and grain from the west coast of South America. These iron sailing ships with their greater length to beam and with all wire rigging could sail closer to the wind than could the wooden vessels. The development of railways across North America opened up faster and more dependable means of transport than vessels sailing around Cape Horn. Then Maritime shipbuilders simply did not go into the building of iron or steel sailing vessels. For centuries their raw materials had been literally growing at their back doors. These builders knew wood and how to work it. When the day of the wooden square-rigger was ending, some would go into the building of the three and four-masted cargo schooners. But not into iron or steel.

It was against this evolving background that the *Glooscap* reached Philadelphia on August 2, 1899 after her 'derelict' voyage and discharged her cargo of sugar. Then she was towed to New York and drydocked for repairs. George Spicer went home for a rest, resuming command in January 1900 in New York for a voyage which would mark the beginning of his own sunset years at sea.

The *Glooscap* had been chartered to Melbourne with a mixed cargo of oil, resin and slate. While the vessel was loading, there was a heavy snowfall in New York and the newspapers reported that 24,000 men and 7,000 carts were employed clearing the streets. The population of the city at the time was about 1,500,000.

The ship sailed on March 2, 1900 and reached Melbourne on June 15. She then proceeded to Newcastle to load coal for Manila, where she arrived on October 11. Spicer was hoping for a charter which would bring him back to New York or Philadelphia. Instead he received a cable from the J.F. Whitney Company ordering the *Glooscap* to proceed to Puget Sound:

> I was knocked out when I got the cable as I did not want to go there and was not expecting such a voyage.

But like it or not, Spicer had no choice and on December 10 the *Glooscap* left Manila on the long passage across the Pacific. On February 14, 1901 the ship moored in Tacoma where she was chartered to load lumber for Melbourne. She sailed on April 4 and arrived in Melbourne on June 20. Her next port was Newcastle, again to load coal for Manila. In Manila orders arrived to sail to Singapore in ballast. The *Glooscap* sailed for Singapore on December 7, 1901 and those on board could not know that exactly forty years later the Japanese would bomb Pearl Harbour with its resulting consequences for a world already at war.

When the ship arrived in Singapore on December 16, it had taken her 142 sailing days to sail from Tacoma to Singpore by way of Melbourne, Newcastle and Manila. Present-day jets fly from Vancouver to Singapore via London and Bombay in less than twenty-two hours.

In Singapore, Spicer finally got the orders he wanted. The *Glooscap* was to load coffee, tapioca and other goods for Boston. She sailed into Boston Harbour on June 24 after a passage of 105 days. It was the last voyage to the Far East for George Spicer.

Part of the cargo was unloaded in Boston then the ship was towed to New York, the destination for the rest of the cargo. When Spicer arrived home in early August 1902, after an absence of two and a half years, 'I found everyone waiting to meet me and all the flags flying.'

20
Three Ships and Their Demise

*I*n August 1903, George Spicer relieved his brother Edmund and took the ship *George T. Hay* on a round voyage from New York to Havre and Rouen, France. The *Hay*, a ship of 1,647 registered tons, had been launched at Spencers Island in 1887 and this was the only voyage on which George Spicer had charge of the vessel. The ship sailed from New York on August 8 and all went well until August 24 when the weather began to deteriorate:

> All the evening and first of the night a very heavy thunder and lightning storm and rain in torrents from 5 p.m. to 9 p.m. Not finished until after midnight. The early part of August 25 dull and gloomy. Moderate S.W. and S.S.W. winds and not much rain. At 4:30 a.m. set royals. At 6 a.m. everything on ship set. Not looking bad at all. 10 a.m. took in all the light sails. 11 a.m. lower fore topsail broke and went all to pieces. Took in upper fore and main topsails. Noon breezing up fast. At noon main lower topsail blew to pieces. By 2 p.m. the gale was something terrific taking everything before it. Foresail split and went to pieces. We just saved some rags. 2:30 p.m. main topmast head broke and everything went overboard. Cut the backstay lanyards and everything necessary to clear the

wreckage. When the spar fell it broke mizzen skysail, royal stays, main crosstrees and the following sails — mainsail, upper topgallant, royal and skysail and broke and lost a lot of wire and chain. Also the blocks, main topgallant, royal and mizzen royal mast. Gale left things a complete wreck. The rail was chafed some, also the side of the ship and other damage. A very high sea.

In short, the *George T. Hay* was a mess. Broken spars, tangled rigging and remnants of sail littered the deck and trailed over the sides of the labouring vessel. By the next day the weather had moderated sufficiently for all hands to begin clearing away the wreckage. The passage continued and on September 5 the ship anchored at Havre. After discharging part of her cargo, the *Hay* was towed up the river to Rouen where the rest of the cargo was unloaded and chalk taken on for New York. The return passage was a boisterous and slow forty-three days from port to port.

Three years later, in March 1906, the *George T. Hay* was carrying hay from Rosario, Argentina to South Africa when she caught fire and had to be abandoned. Her master, Edmund Spicer, and the officers and crew were picked up by a Norwegian barque and landed at Port Elizabeth, South Africa.

During 1904 George Spicer and the J.F. Whitney Company had been attempting to sell the *Charles S. Whitney*. The ship was now nineteen years old, repairs were costly and freights increasingly scarce for the aging vessel. In early December Spicer was able to write:

The *Charles S. Whitney* left the wharf for Staten Island in care of J.B. King's men. We are out of her altogether. I was sorry to see her go in one way and glad in another. She is a good ship and at one time was a good property but there is no business for her now so old friends must part.

The *Whitney* was cut down into a gypsum barge, renamed the *Lewis H. St. John* and remained in that service until the 1920s when she was worn out.

In 1910 the *Glooscap* joined the *Charles S. Whitney* in the fleet of gypsum barges. Fourteen years later, in 1924, she was sunk as a result of a collision in New York Harbour. As the wreck was considered a menace to navigation, divers were sent down in July 1931 and planted explosives. They blew the top off the old vessel and her cargo of gypsum spewed into the harbour. A number of her timbers remained and these were pulled up, put on a lighter and taken out to sea and sunk. Thus the last of the big ships from the Parrsboro shore disappeared from the scene.

The demise of the Spencers Island vessels is typical of the end of the thousands of square-rigged vessels which were produced in Maritime shipyards. If some, like the *J.F. Whitney* and *E.J. Spicer* ended their days under foreign flags, others were abandoned at sea, consumed by fire or wrecked on faraway shores. A few, when their day was done, were simply hauled out on a beach and burned for their metal or left to disintegrate. Whatever the means, one by one they all went.

21
Wages and Dividends

*N*o story of a master mariner would be complete without some mention of his income in relation to his time and occupation.

Master mariners from the Maritime provinces did not usually accumulate any great wealth but most enjoyed a comfortable way of life. There are still many large houses in the seaside towns and villages of these provinces, houses built and owned by nineteenth century sea captains, which stand as testimonials to their standard of living.

Captain George Spicer received $600 per year as a master when he took command of the *Globe* in 1868. Ten years later his wages increased to $1,000 annually. Still later they rose to $1,200, the most he would ever receive during his years at sea.

A major portion of the income of these men came from their investments, largely in shares in the vessels they sailed as well as in other vessels.

In the earlier years of his career, dividends received by Captain Spicer from shares he owned in the *J.F. Whitney* and *E.J. Spicer* are summarized by the following examples:

1876	6 shares	$ 677.97
1879	8 shares	842.01
1881	28 shares	1,441.60
1883	28 shares	2,290.33

But, in case this presents an unduly favourable picture of income, it must be noted that in periods of economic slumps, when charters were less frequent and freight rates were down, dividends also dropped markedly.

It may also be noted that in 1884, as an example, George Spicer was paying $3.25 for a ton of coal, 6½¢ per pound of fresh beef, 50¢ for a bushel of potatoes and $2.25 for a barrel of apples from the Annapolis Valley. At the end of 1884 the entire household expenses for the Spicer family of seven were $1,300, 'The largest for any year since we have been married.'

When Captain Spicer took the *Charles S. Whitney* to sea in 1885 on her maiden voyage, the ship's complement and the monthly wages were:

Captain	$100	Carpenter	$30
Mate	45	Ten able seamen @	25
Cook/Steward	40	Three ordinary seamen @	10
Second Mate	32	Cabin Boy	9

Seven years later, when Spicer was sailing the *Glooscap*, the monthly wages were nearly identical.

In 1903 the cumulative dividends paid by each vessel in which Spicer then had an interest totalled:

Charles S. Whitney	launched 1885	$100,905.44
George T. Hay	launched 1887	107,363.52
Glooscap	launched 1891	74,112.48

A conservative estimate of George Spicer's share of these dividends for the eighteen years would be $30,000.

Over the years Spicer also had other investments. He owned shares in three of the schooners built at Spencers Island and in one of the square-riggers built in Kingsport, N.S. He was a shareholder in the New York Sailmaking Company and in an axe factory in St. Stephen, N.B., managed by his son-in-law. And he was an early investor in Nova Scotia Telephone stock.

All in all he supported his family of seven, sent three of his children on to a post-high school education and lived for twenty-seven years in comfortable retirement — long before the era of old age pensions.

22

The Family at Sea

*T*he families of nineteenth century master mariners frequently went to sea with their husbands and fathers. It was not uncommon for young boys and girls to have seen much of the world before they first set foot inside a school.

Five children were born to George and Emily Jane Spicer: Minnie in 1871, Percy in 1873, Gertrude in 1874 and then two more sons, Whitney in 1880 and Stanley in 1882. All were taken to sea at various times and Whitney lost his life at sea.

On board ship the younger children would play, much like they would at home, limited only by the more confined quarters of a vessel. When young Stanley was taken to Shanghai in 1888, one of the last items taken on board the ship was a tricycle. On July 31 Emily noted:

> Today is Whitney and Stanley's birthday. Whitney is 8 and Stanley 6. I don't know how Whitney spent his but Stanley's was celebrated with all ceremony. George fired six rounds from his new gun. The steward and mates also fired a salute. The steward made him a blueberry pie and gave him one dollar for a present.

On the next voyage to Shanghai, George and Emily took their fifteen-year-old daughter Gertrude. Much of the ladies' time was taken up with sewing and knitting. As the voyage neared its end Emily was able to write:

> Gertie finished her quilt and we have listed all the sewing and knitting we have done and there are pages of them. Sheets and underwear, drésses, wrappers, shirts, fancy work and all sorts of wearable and household goods. We planned out our voyage and we finished the work.

When family members were on board, they were nearly always accompanied by a pet, usually a cat or a canary. Often these pets came to an untimely end, the cats sometimes fell overboard and sometimes there were other accidents:

> At 9:30 a.m. Minnie stepped on little Dick (the canary bird) and killed him instantly. We was all very sorry. He was such a nice bird and a splendid singer.

Living on board ship inevitably brought family members into contact with many aspects of seafaring including relationships between officers and crew. George Spicer succinctly mentioned one such incident when the *Glooscap* was in Manila:

> In the morning two of the men would not go to work. Took one to the Consul's office and charged him with insubordination. Put the other one in irons after he threatened to cut the guts out of me.

The son of Captain George Stailing once related an incident which happened while his father was sailing the *Savona* from Calcutta to Boston. Captain Stailing had his wife and two sons with him on the voyage:

> We had picked up a hard-case crew in India who gave a lot of trouble. One day in the tropics, my brother and I were listening to mother reading aloud from a book and my father was pacing the poop. There was a large bewhiskered sailor going through the motions of

caulking a seam on the poop and my father noticed the way the fellow was 'sojering on the job' and he admonished him. The sailor, in a burst of rage, leaped to his feet and made a swing at father with the caulking mallet. Had the blow struck home, there was no telling what might have happened, but Dad sidestepped the attack and closed with the sailor, and before we youngsters knew it almost, he had the sailor down on the deck. The man was quickly ironed and confined until we reached Boston.

Young Stailing made several voyages with his father but this was the only occasion when he ever saw him lift his hand to a man.

The wives and children of captains who spent any amount of time at sea were bound to see and hear flare-ups between officers and crew as well as watch their vessel being pounded by gales and heavy seas. It all went with life on board ship.

In port the Spicer children had many opportunities to widen their horizons and expand their knowledge. In London they were taken to see the Tower of London, Westminster, Buckingham Palace and Madam Tussaud's Wax Works. They visited zoological gardens and attended concerts. In Shanghai Stanley and Gertrude went for rides on rickshaws. Always there was shopping and the home of George and Emily Spicer was filled with the furniture, dishes and other acquisitions brought back from the voyages.

Emily found plenty to occupy her time when at sea. She had her sewing and knitting as well as the usual housework of washing, ironing and cleaning for the family. If the meals were normally provided by the cook and steward, occasionally Emily took a turn in the galley. On one of their voyages to Shanghai the cook complained of the stale flour they had purchased in port. Emily went in the galley and made bread. She concluded the fault lay with the cook rather than with the flour.

On the passage from Shanghai to Ilo Ilo in the Philippines in 1888, Emily described the menus for two days on board the ship:

Sunday — **Breakfast:** Ham and eggs (when the hens lay), herring, bread and butter and tea. **Dinner:** Oyster stew, potatoes and canned meat, plum duff, bread and butter, tea or lime juice and water. **Supper:** Brown bread, beans, sweet breads or cakes, canned fruit and tea.

Monday — **Breakfast:** Codfish and potatoes, bread and butter and tea. **Dinner:** Bean soup, potatoes and beef, bread and butter, apple pie and lime juice with water to drink. **Supper:** Not listed.

The sail to Ilo Ilo was only of eleven days' duration so the meals were somewhat more sumptuous than on the longer passage from New York to Shanghai. It was evident that on the New York to Shanghai run, the provisions were becoming a bit thin for, as they neared the China coast, Emily wrote:

> I want some potatoes and fresh meat almost as bad as letters from home. I expect if I got both at once I would eat a potato before I read the letters.

Sundays at sea were observed in that the only work undertaken was that necessary to keep the ship operational. On one of their voyages to the Far East, Emily went a step further when sailing from Shanghai to Hong Kong:

> **Sunday** — At 4 p.m. Emily invited all the crew that wanted to come so eight of them came aft and had some singing. Gertie played the organ. Then we all read a verse, about one chapter in all from the New Testament. Emily talked to them a little — all of which took about 45 minutes.

It was a program which Emily followed on succeeding Sundays throughout the voyage back to New York.

The children of master mariners usually went to school in their own towns or villages, staying with relatives if both parents were at sea. There was, however, one school which played an important role in the education of many sons of sea captains, a school which both Whitney and Stanley Spicer attended.

Acacia Villa School at Hortonville, near Wolfville, Nova Scotia was a private residential school founded in 1852 for boys, especially the sons of master mariners who took their wives to sea. The boys were mostly between nine and nineteen and they undertook an academic program that prepared them for university entrance as well as emphasizing commerce, music and elocution. Particular attention was placed on spelling, handwriting, promptness and good behaviour. The Acacia Villa School was in some ways ahead of its time as its facilities included a gymnasium, sports field, library and a science laboratory. The students led a spartan existence and the faculty was never accused of sparing the rod to spoil the child. Acacia Villa closed its doors in 1920 but in the sixty-eight years of its existence hundreds of boys passed through its doors including such luminaries as Robert Laird Borden, later a Prime Minister of Canada; Allister Fraser, a future Lieutenant-Governor of Nova Scotia; and Isaac Walton Killam, the business tycoon and philanthropist.

When the children remained at home, much of their lives, especially for the boys, revolved around the local shipyard. Not long before his own death many years later, Stanley looked back:

> All the fun boys can know in a shipyard was ours. Always we could spot a mistake in the rigging of a ship of our period. We watched the vessels come and go. We knew the strong ties of family separated by long months, even years, on the sea. A letter was mailed at every port of call for the next ship to pick up to bring back to the little port on the Bay. Much could happen at home or on the sea between reunions. We played in the lumber yard where the man with the adze worked patiently. We saw the logs cut in the woods not far away. We rode the sleds bringing the timbers out and rowed the little boats as soon as we could hold an oar. We chewed tar and learned to sew with palm and needle. There was plenty to occupy a healthy boy in a shipbuilding village in the days of wooden ships.

And when the family stayed at home and it was time for Captain Spicer to return to sea, the partings were always hard: 'I felt very bad leaving home to see them all in tears. I could not keep the tears out of my own eyes.' But farewells were part of a seafarer's life.

23

The Captain at Sea —
Some Vignettes

*I*f the captain of a sailing vessel had to fulfill the combined roles of navigator, negotiator, business man and authoritarian, his work at sea ranged from facing instant crisis to the mundane task of wielding a paint brush.

Sometimes even the sanctuary of ports provided their own unique experiences and Captain George Spicer had his share. There were quarantines to be endured in some ports; pilots who managed to put vessels aground; crews that ran away, particularly in the late days of sail; and the ever-present danger of collisions in crowded harbours.

Captain Spicer wrote of one such incident when he cleared London in the *Charles S. Whitney*. It was June 19, 1886:

> This day a moderate breeze to moderate gale from N.W. to north with rain from 4 to 6 p.m. then cloudy, some showers and heavy squalls all the rest of the day. The pilot came on board and at 2 a.m. the tug *Red Rose* arrived. We commenced to tow down the river. Got to Gravesend about 5:45 a.m. Took pilot F.H. Dains on board and proceeded towards the Downs. I was fully intending to proceed to sea at once but the tide was turning and the wind was from the N.W. to N.N.W. Several vessels outside appeared to be not fetching down and the pilot advised against it. I decided to

anchor until the tide turned. At 1 p.m. anchored and the pilot left. 3:30 p.m. commenced to heave up the anchor but it blowed so hard we could hardly get the anchor. Only had forty feet of chain out altogether. At 5 p.m. the anchor broke away and run the jib up. But the ship did not pay off as much as I expected and before we could get the anchor so she would pay off quickly, she struck the old brig *Laura* of Southampton and carried away nearly everything on board (the *Laura*) but the foremast and bowsprit. Most of the other spars went over the side but did not hurt the hull and only broke a small piece of the rail and bulwarks. The *Red Rose* towed the brig away. It was the first collision I was ever in.

The *Whitney* proceeded to sea and Captain Spicer entered the incident in the ship's log. Later, on arrival in New York, a settlement was reached with the owners of the *Laura* by a payment to them of £300.

At sea, when weather permitted, the captain took daily sights, plotted his vessel's position, and kept the ship's log up to date. If the vessel was carrying a potentially dangerous cargo, such as hay or coal, there were regular inspections of the cargo, for fire on board a wooden windship was one of the greatest hazards feared by captain and crew.

Decisions on sail changing were the captain's responsibility and these could be frequent as illustrated by two excerpts from Spicer's journal when he was sailing the brig *Globe* from New York to Liverpool, England in 1871:

> **November 18** — First of the day moderate breeze S.E. and cloudy. Latter part moderate gale S.S.E. to south and squalls of rain. 8 p.m. tacked ship and took in light sails. 11 p.m. took in topgallant sails. 2 a.m. reefed topsails and took in flying jib. 5 a.m. took in mainsail. 8 a.m. tacked ship.
> **November 21** — First of this day strong gale S.S.W. with very heavy squalls. 8 p.m. wind moderated and hauled S.W. Wore ship, set foresail and trysail, upper main topsail. 2 a.m. set upper fore topsail, mainsail and jib. 3 a.m. set topgallants and royals.

These few notations also indicate that hours of the day or night meant nothing when a vessel was underway.

The treatment of injuries at sea depended on whatever skills the shipmaster possessed and the rudimentary contents of the ship's medicine chest. Infections, fevers, broken bones and burns were among the maladies encountered. Spicer described one incident in 1874:

> This day commences with a violent gale W.S.W. with a tremendous sea. The cook had his back scalded, the medicine chest upset and broke some bottles. The second mate will do the cooking and I will stand his watch.

The typical medicine chest of the time contained such materials as: bitter tincture, bark powder, flux powder, castor oil, eye wash, Goulard's Extract, oil of turpentine, extract of peppermint, rubber cement, burgundy pitch, a packet of gold thread for sore mouths, pain killer, Simpson's Diarrhoea Cordial, Johnson's Liniment, bicarbonate of soda, cream of tartar, Friar's Balsam, laudanum, salve, alum, safety pins, a spoon, small knife and apothecaries' weights. Each bottle was numbered and included in the chest was a small book entitled, *The Guide Book To The Government Medicine Chest For Merchant Seamen.* It was published in London in 1852.

The nineteenth century vessels carried slop chests and the slops consisted of such items as clothing, tobacco and other materials which seamen and officers might require on voyages. Part of Captain Spicer's ritual in each port was the purchase of goods for the slop chest. The men purchasing the goods had the costs deducted from their wages.

When the *Charles S. Whitney* was being readied for a voyage to Shanghai, Spicer laid in slops at a cost of $572.54. At the end of the voyage there was just $43 worth of goods left. One ordinary seaman's purchases, charged against his wages of ten dollars a month are examples of the kinds of goods purchased and their cost:

cap	30¢	knife	25¢
singlet	60¢	straw hat	25¢
pair of drawers	65¢	cap (second hand)	25¢

knife	35¢	2 tins of milk	30¢
1 lb. tobacco	50¢	cash advance	$1.00
mosquito netting	15¢	shirt	$2.00

In all his years as a master mariner, George Spicer only mentioned one occasion when he carried passengers. In 1886 when he sailed from London to New York he had two lady passengers on board. It was an unhappy experience on all sides. The crossing was a long and stormy passage in mid-winter. Both ladies were seasick from the day they left port and daily, sometimes hourly, they wanted to know how far they were from New York. When the ship finally docked and Spicer took the ladies to board a train he was vastly relieved, 'I don't know when I was so pleased to get clear of any people.' It was a feeling, no doubt, fervently reciprocated by the ladies.

At sea the captain regularly worked alongside the men. Like shipmasters of his time, George Spicer was proficient with palm and needle and he helped to repair torn sails and cut out and sew new ones. On new vessels, Spicer usually waited for the maiden voyage when he would make canvas covers for the ship's boats and awnings for the after decks. Often it was the captain who painted his own cabin and other rooms in the after quarters.

Nova Scotia master mariners took particular pride in the appearance of their vessels. The vessels not only had to be seaworthy in all respects, they had to *appear* shipshape and smart. When a vessel was nearing port, all hands were turned to and cleaning and painting were the orders of the day. In July 1909 the *Glooscap* had departed Buenos Aires and as the ship neared Barbados, preparations were made for the vessel's arrival in port:

> **August 7** — Moderate gale S.S.E. with heavy squalls of wind and rain until after daylight when it cleared. By afternoon wind had gone E.S.E. and very fine weather. We could smell the land but could not see anything. Ship made about 240 miles, was going from 8 to 11 knots. All sail set from 8 a.m. Crew employed cleaning paint. I mixed a hundred pounds of paint.

August 8 — Fresh breeze from S.E. round to E.N.E. by 6 p.m. Beautiful fine weather all day and a smooth sea. Ship going 8 and 9 knots. Made 215 miles. Thermometer 78⁰F. At noon seen a small coastal schooner standing in to the land. 8 a.m. seen the land, low sandy shore and high land back. All sail set that would draw.

August 9 — Moderate breeze from E.N.E. to S.E. most of the time and very fine weather all day. Crew commenced to tar the rigging. All the cleaning done ready for painting as soon as dry enough. Crossed the Line today in Longitude 43⁰W.

August 10 — Light breeze from the E.N.E. to E.S.E. Very fine weather all day. Ship going from 5 to 8 knots and made 210 miles. Had a strong current W.N.W. Crew finished tarring down the rigging and commenced a little painting. I had a man to work finishing repairs on the old topgallant sail that got torn up.

August 11 — Light breeze from the E.N.E. and fine all day. Ship going from one to 6 knots. Thermometer 80⁰F. All hands to work painting. Got all done on the poop and a lot on the main deck. I was to work getting paint ready and doing some painting.

August 12 — Moderate breeze from S.S.E. Fine weather. Ship going from 2 to 6 knots. Made 128 miles. Thermometer 83⁰F. Nothing to be seen at all. All hands to work painting. Got all the white paint on, a first coat and all the blocks painted. I was painting the names on the boats and wheel cover besides keeping the paint ready for the men.

When the *Glooscap* reached port on August 21, she was in pristine condition.

24

The Final Years

*T*he last five years of George Spicer's seafaring career were spent in a succession of voyages to South America and to ports in the Caribbean and Gulf of Mexico. They were difficult years in that charters for the *Glooscap* were increasingly hard to find and the quality of crews had deteriorated to a marked degree. Time and again Spicer would note at the beginning of a voyage:

> Found that a good many of the crew of would-be sailors can do scarcely anything — steer or anything else. It took all of them to furl a sail.

Invariably once the ship reached port many of the crew would run away. They were either looking for cheap transportation from one port to another or getting out one step ahead of the law.

And at sea there were more and more disciplinary problems. Numerous times Captain Spicer had to put unruly sailors in irons until they cooled off. Sometimes it was his officers:

> The second mate was in his room and would not work. He was also very cheeky. I threw him out on deck. Disrated him and put him in the forecastle. The

next day he was very sick from drinking bay rum but recovered and went to work.

During his years as a shipmaster, George Spicer cooperated with the United States Government in gathering information. Regularly on his voyages bottles were thrown overboard which contained forms on which the vessel reported her name, position, date and ocean current in that position. If the bottle was picked up by another vessel, the position was noted and the form forwarded to the U.S. Navy Department in Washington. Over time the procedure helped in gaining increased knowledge of currents in the world's oceans.

In his last years, sailing to the south, the emphasis was on taking water temperatures at various positions and these too were regularly reported to the Navy Department. Before he retired George Spicer was presented with a barometer by the U.S. Navy for his faithful reporting of currents, water temperatures and other data.

If Spicer had troubles with charters and crews, there were compensations from time to time. August 1907 found the *Glooscap* at La Brea, Trinidad to load pitch. George and Janetta were taken to see Pitch Lake:

> Quite a wonder in itself. Rather lower than the surrounding country. The tubs of pitch are filled in the lake, brought on a trolley car, put on a wire and taken to the ship a little over a mile away. We were told the lake settles six inches for every 100,000 tons taken out.

And, two years later when the ship was moored at Sabine Pass, Texas, the ship's agent arranged an automobile ride for George and Janetta. It was a first and the Spicers were indeed moving into the twentieth century.

In early 1909 the *Glooscap* again made the news. On February 17 the vessel left Barbados for Boston in ballast and by early March gales and high seas were encountered. The ship arrived in Boston on March 9 and the next day an account of her passage appeared in a Boston newspaper:

> After a boisterous passage of three weeks from Barbados (B.W.I.), the British ship *Glooscap* of

Parrsboro, N.S., Captain George D. Spicer, was towed up the harbour yesterday afternoon by the tug *Orion* which picked her up off Highland Light early yesterday morning.

There was little in the appearance of the ship to indicate that she had been fighting against furious storms for 1,800 miles. Thursday night (March 4) the *Glooscap* was struck by a gale followed by a terrific electrical storm during which the yards and rigging were aglow. Heavy thunder and vivid lightning continued throughout the night.

Mrs. Spicer who has accompanied her husband on every passage he has made during the past twelve years was not in the least alarmed during the storm which hammered the ship. She is used to the tempests and she rather enjoys rough weather.

The *Glooscap* left Campbellton (N.B.) July 18 last with 1,500,000 feet of lumber for Buenos Aires. After delivery of the cargo she went to Barbados where she lay seven weeks before she received orders to proceed to Boston. In her holds she had 450 tons of copper dross for ballast. The vessel will commence to take on a cargo of lumber for Buenos Aires.

On June 14, 1910 the *Glooscap* sailed from La Brea with another cargo of pitch. It would be her last voyage as a full-rigged ship. The vessel arrived in New York on July 1 and Spicer noted the arrival:

> 1:30 p.m. got the tug *Hercules* off Seabright to tow us to Staten Island for $100. Anchored at 10 p.m. A reporter on board. Got all the sails unbent and put away.

The *Glooscap* had been sold to the J.B. King Company and her destiny lay as a barge, freighting gypsum between Windsor, N.S. and New York. In this trade she would be joining a number of fine old windships she had known in many of the world's ports including her sister-ship, the *Charles S. Whitney*; the *Ontario* and *Plymouth*, both Hantsport-built vessels; the old *Wildwood* out of Saint John; and Yarmouth County's *Lizzie Burrill* among them. As for George Spicer — on July 19, 1910 he wrote:

> At 3 p.m. a tugboat came and towed the *Glooscap* to Mariner's Harbour, Staten Island. After she was moored and everything in shape I received a cheque in payment for the ship from J.B. King and Company. I locked the doors and felt bad about leaving the ship.

A seagoing career spanning fifty-two years had come to an end and retirement was at hand.

Epilogue

*C*aptain George D. Spicer was not quite through with the sea. In August 1911 he agreed to relieve his brother Edmund, master of the three-masted schooner *Coral Leaf*. George took the *Coral Leaf* from Spencers Island to New York with piling and brought her back in ballast. It was not an experience he enjoyed, 'I do not think much of schooners to go to sea in, too much rolling and slatting.' It had been nearly half a century since he had last sailed a schooner and over the years he had become a square-rigger man through and through.

Nor had he seen the last of all of his old vessels. Nearly a dozen barques and ships, their masts and rigging cut down, were freighting gypsum from Windsor, N.S. to New York. These barges were loaded near Windsor then towed by small tugs to Spencers Island where an ocean tug picked them up for the passage to New York. When empty, the barges were towed back to Spencers Island where the smaller tugs took them on to Windsor. Thus for years after he left the sea Captain Spicer would often see his old ships the *Charles S. Whitney*, now the *Lewis H. St. John*, and the *Glooscap* anchored off in the bay. They were no longer the lofty windships he had once commanded, now they were little more than hulls on the end of a towline. Occasionally he would board one just to see her again. But not often.

In the years that were left to him, George Spicer busied himself with his woodlot, garden and property. Like many retired seamen of the time, he kept his house and grounds in meticulous order, painted, neat, the fences regularly whitewashed and everything shipshape. Frequently he substituted for the local postmistress, he was secretary of the Spencers Island school trustees and he continued his interest in the little Union Church he had helped bring to reality back in 1882. For several years he was the local collector of customs and, as such, entered and cleared all vessels that came in to Spencers Island. 'It kept my hand in,' he used to say.

By 1928 many of the captains of the square-rigged vessels had gone and those left were well along in years. That year George, his brother Dewis, and three other master mariners from along the shore had a get-together. George carefully noted that their combined ages totalled four hundred eight years and five months.

Time was taking its toll within his own family. In February 1915 his mother passed away at ninety. One by one his brothers and sisters followed. Of the nine children who grew to adulthood, George, the eldest, outlived them all except for one sister in Saskatchewan and his youngest sister Blanche, twenty-three years his junior. Janetta died in 1932 and once again the captain was a widower.

Then on September 21, 1937, thirteen days past his ninety-first birthday, life left George Dimock Spicer. He was buried beside his beloved Emily Jane in the Advocate Cemetery, less than two miles from where he had been born. He had come full circle.

There is no epitaph over his grave, he wanted none, but surely the words of Robert Louis Stevenson would have been fitting:

Here he lies where he longed to be;
Home is the sailor, home from sea.

Appendix

Known Voyages of Captain George D. Spicer
1871-1910

*W*hile fairly detailed information remains on most of the voyages of Captain Spicer from the time he received his master's papers in 1868 until he retired in 1910, there are some gaps. There is little to describe his activities from 1868 to 1871 and for occasional years thereafter, the records have simply disappeared. The remaining data, however, serve to illustrate the kinds of voyages and cargoes carried in his vessels, typical of the times.

It should be noted that the dates of arrivals and departures are from port to port. When vessels left a harbour, they took their departure from a recognized point such as a cape, buoy or light. Similarly, when they arrived at a port, they ceased their sea log outside the harbour. Port to port times included towing into a harbour or up a river and thus are almost always longer than recorded sea times for a voyage.

An examination of the following list will reveal lengthy stays in port. Occasionally a vessel would be directed to a port for orders and these orders would be slow in coming. More often it was due to the loading and unloading methods of the times. Sawn lumber was handled a plank at a time and bagged cargoes were handled a bag at a time. If the vessel was alongside a dock, the cargo arrived or was carried away by horse and cart. If the vessel was anchored off, cargoes were ferried by small lighters operating on uncertain schedules. In many ports stevedores worked at a leisurely pace, holidays were numerous and strikes common. And, sometimes, vessels simply had to wait for charters. The turn-around schedule of the modern freighter was a long way in the future.

Vessel	From	Destination	Cargo
		1871	
Brig Globe	Not Known (departed late 1870)	Trinidad De Cuba (arrived January 11)	Coal
Brig Globe	Trinidad De Cuba (departed January 27)	Queenstown, Ireland (arrived April 4)	360 Tons Sugar
Brig Globe	Queenstown, Ireland (departed May 15)	Boston (arrived June 21)	384 Tons Iron and Pipe
Brig Globe	Boston (departed July 1)	Spencers Island (arrived July 4)	Ballast
Brig Globe	Spencers Island (departed July 5)	Kingsport, N.S. (arrived July 5)	Ballast. Vessel hauled for repairs.
Brig Globe	Kingsport, N.S. (departed July 12)	Black Rock, N.S. (arrived July 12)	Ballast
Brig Globe	Black Rock, N.S. (departed July 17)	Boston (arrived August 8)	510 Tons Gypsum
Brig Globe	Boston (departed August 20)	Spencers Island (arrived August 28)	Ballast
Brig Globe	Spencers Island (departed August 30)	Kingsport, N.S. (arrived August 30)	Ballast. Vessel hauled for repairs.
Brig Globe	Kingsport, N.S. (departed September 18)	Spencers Island (arrived September 22)	Loaded gypsum en-route at Black Rock

Brig Globe	Spencers Island (departed September 26)	New York (arrived October 3)	517 Tons Gypsum
Brig Globe	New York (departed October 21)	Liverpool, England (arrived November 24)	Petroleum

1872

Brig Globe	Liverpool, England (departed January 11)	Bahia, Argentina (arrived March 12)	Coal
Brig Globe	Bahia, Argentina (departed May 14)	Antwerp (arrived July 15)	Cotton and Sugar

Captain Spicer left the *Globe* in Antwerp and returned to Spencers Island where he helped finish the new barque *J.F. Whitney*. The vessel was launched December 3, 1872.

Barque J.F. Whitney	Spencers Island (departed December 8)	Saint John, N.B. (arrived December 8)	Ballast

1873

No Records Available

1874

Barque J.F. Whitney	Not Known	New York (arrived late 1873)	Pumice Stone, Baled Rags and Marble

Barque J.F. Whitney	New York (departed March 12)	Liverpool, England (arrived April 1)	Naptha and Oil
Barque J.F. Whitney	Liverpool, England (departed April 28)	Sydney, N.S. (arrived May 24)	Ballast
Barque J.F. Whitney	Sydney, N.S. (departed June 16)	Montreal (arrived June 21)	Coal
Barque J.F. Whitney	Montreal (departed July 20)	Queenstown, Ireland (arrived August 8 for orders)	Corn
Barque J.F. Whitney	Queenstown, Ireland (departed September 1)	Hull, England (arrived September 7)	Corn
Barque J.F. Whitney	Hull (under tow) (departed September 21)	North Shields, England (arrived September 22)	Ballast
Barque J.F. Whitney	North Shields (departed October 24)	New York (arrived December 5)	Soda Ash, Baled Rags, Bleaching Powder

1875

No Records Available

1876

| Barque J.F. Whitney | New York (departed January 24) | Antwerp (arrived February 15) | Crude Oil and Staves |
| Barque J.F. Whitney | Antwerp (departed March 21) | New York (arrived April 24) | Glass, Marble, Empty Barrels |

111

Barque J.F. Whitney	New York (departed June 8)	London (arrived July 5)	Crude Oil
Barque J.F. Whitney	London (departed July 19)	New York (arrived August 23)	Ballast
Barque J.F. Whitney	New York (departed September 9)	Rotterdam (arrived October 6)	Crude Oil
Barque J.F. Whitney	Rotterdam (departed October 28)	New York (arrived November 18)	Empty Barrels
Barque J.F. Whitney	New York (departed December 23)	London (arrived January 9, 1877)	Crude Oil

1877

Barque J.F. Whitney	London (departed January 23)	New York (arrived March 3)	Ballast
Barque J.F. Whitney	New York (departed May 10)	Rotterdam (arrived June 1)	Crude Oil
Barque J.F. Whitney	Rotterdam (departed June 24)	New York (arrived August 4)	4,100 Empty Barrels
Barque J.F. Whitney	New York (departed September 1)	Havre, France (arrived October 9)	Naptha
Barque J.F. Whitney	Havre, France (departed October 24)	New York (arrived December 3)	Ballast

Captain Spicer was home from December 1877 until he
rejoined the vessel in New York in March 1878.

1878

Barque J.F. Whitney	New York (departed March 19)	Liverpool, England (arrived April 9)	4,387 Barrels Refined Oil
Barque J.F. Whitney	Liverpool, England (departed April 27)	New York (arrived May 22)	Ballast
Barque J.F. Whitney	New York (departed June 8)	Liverpool, England (arrived July 4)	5,654 Barrels Naptha
Barque J.F. Whitney	Liverpool, England (departed July 19)	New York (arrived August 21)	Ballast
Barque J.F. Whitney	New York (departed September 14)	Rotterdam (arrived October 8)	4,400 Barrels Refined Oil
Barque J.F. Whitney	Rotterdam (departed November 5)	New York (arrived December 5)	3,825 Empty Barrels
Barque J.F. Whitney	New York (departed December 25)	Bordeaux, France (arrived January 11, 1879)	5,716 Barrels Naptha and Crude Oil

1879

Barque J.F. Whitney	Bordeaux, France (departed February 25)	New York (arrived March 22)	Ballast

113

Barque J.F. Whitney	New York (departed April 8)	Caibarien, Cuba (arrived April 20)	No charters in New York. To Cuba on Speculation.
Barque J.F. Whitney	Caibarien, Cuba (departed May 28)	Boston (arrived June 6)	1,000 Hogsheads Sugar
Barque J.F. Whitney	Boston (departed July 3)	Rotterdam (arrived July 24)	Oil
Barque J.F. Whitney	Rotterdam (departed August 23)	New York (arrived October 3)	Iron and Empty Barrels
Barque J.F. Whitney	New York (departed October 25)	Havre, France (arrived November 17)	Crude Oil
Barque J.F. Whitney	Havre, France (departed December 2)	New York (arrived December 30)	Ballast

1880

Barque J.F. Whitney	New York (departed January 23)	Amsterdam (arrived February 13)	Oil
Barque J.F. Whitney	Amsterdam (departed March 21)	New York (arrived April 22)	Iron Rails, Baled Rags, Empty Barrels

Captain Spicer turned the *J.F. Whitney* over to his brother Dewis and returned home. Ship *E.J. Spicer* launched November 17. The ship registered 1,317 tons and cost $47,042 complete.

Ship	Departed	Arrived	Cargo
Ship E.J. Spicer	Spencers Island (departed November 26)	Norfolk, Virginia (arrived December 3)	Ballast

1881

Ship	Departed	Arrived	Cargo
Ship E.J. Spicer	Norfolk, Virginia (departed January 14)	Liverpool, England (arrived February 3)	4,685 Bales of Cotton and Mixed Cargo
Ship E.J. Spicer	Liverpool, England (departed February 19)	New York (arrived March 11)	Ballast
Ship E.J. Spicer	New York (departed April 20)	London (arrived May 14)	8,376 Barrels Refined Oil
Ship E.J. Spicer	London (departed May 31)	New York (arrived July 8)	Ballast
Ship E.J. Spicer	New York (departed August 9)	London (arrived August 30)	Refined Oil
Ship E.J. Spicer	London (departed September 21)	New York (arrived October 22)	1,000 Tons Chalk
Ship E.J. Spicer	New York (departed December 2)	Liverpool, England (arrived December 24)	Refined Oil

1882

Ship	Departed	Arrived	Cargo
Ship E.J. Spicer	Liverpool, England (departed January 27)	New York (arrived March 4)	1,396 Tons Salt

Ship	Departed	Arrived	Cargo
Ship E.J. Spicer	New York (departed April 19)	London (arrived May 10)	8,479 Barrels Refined Oil
Ship E.J. Spicer	London (departed May 31)	New York (arrived July 9)	Chalk, Baled Rags and Paper
Ship E.J. Spicer	New York (departed August 7)	London (arrived August 30)	Refined Oil
Ship E.J. Spicer	London (departed September 22)	New York (arrived October 24)	Chalk and Empty Barrels
Ship E.J. Spicer	New York (departed November 27)	Liverpool, England (arrived December 21)	8,411 Barrels Refined Oil

1883

Ship	Departed	Arrived	Cargo
Ship E.J. Spicer	Liverpool, England (departed January 13)	New York (arrived March 7)	439 Tons Salt
Ship E.J. Spicer	New York (departed April 2)	Liverpool, England (arrived April 26)	Refined Oil
Ship E.J. Spicer	Liverpool, England (departed May 28)	New York (arrived June 26)	Soda Ash, Beer, Baled Rags, Empty Barrels
Ship E.J. Spicer	New York (departed August 6)	Antwerp (arrived September 1)	8,545 Barrels Refined Oil
Ship E.J. Spicer	Antwerp (departed September 28)	New York (arrived October 23)	Iron, Wire, Cement, Empty Barrels

| Ship E.J. Spicer | New York (departed November 15) | Liverpool, England (arrived December 10) | Refined Oil |

1884

Ship E.J. Spicer	Liverpool, England (departed January 15)	New York (arrived March 1)	Bleaching Powder, Soda Ash
Ship E.J. Spicer	New York (departed April 4)	Antwerp (arrived May 1)	Refined Oil
Ship E.J. Spicer	Antwerp (departed May 31)	New York (arrived July 12)	Steel Rails, Mineral Water

Captain Spicer returned home in August and remained home for a year helping to finish the new ship *Charles S. Whitney*. The *Whitney* measured 1,651 registered tons and was launched July 14, 1885. Dewis Spicer took command of the *E.J. Spicer*.

1885

| Ship Charles S. Whitney | Spencers Island (departed August 25) | Liverpool, England (arrived September 14) | Lumber |
| Ship Charles S. Whitney | Liverpool, England (departed October 12) | New York (arrived November 2) | Soda Ash |

Ship	Departed	Arrived	Cargo
Ship Charles S. Whitney	New York (departed December 10)	London (arrived December 30)	11,320 Barrels Refined Oil

1886

Ship	Departed	Arrived	Cargo
Ship Charles S. Whitney	London (departed January 28)	New York (arrived March 21)	1,200 Tons Chalk, 7,123 Empty Barrels
Ship Charles S. Whitney	New York (departed May 3)	London (arrived May 26)	11,345 Barrels Refined Oil
Ship Charles S. Whitney	London (departed June 19)	New York (arrived August 6)	802 Tons Cement, 8,000 Empty Barrels
Ship Charles S. Whitney	New York (departed September 11)	Antwerp (arrived October 10)	11,557 Barrels Refined Oil
Ship Charles S. Whitney	Antwerp (departed November 21)	New York (arrived December 26)	Wire and Empty Barrels

1887

Ship	Departed	Arrived	Cargo
Ship Charles S. Whitney	New York (departed January 29)	London (arrived February 22)	11,506 Barrels Refined Oil
Ship Charles S. Whitney	London (departed March 19)	New York (arrived April 17)	Iron Rails, Cement, Empty Barrels
Ship Charles S. Whitney	New York (departed June 2)	London (arrived July 5)	11,582 Barrels Refined Oil

Ship Charles S. Whitney	London (departed July 31) — New York (arrived September 1)	1,540 Tons Cement, 6,000 Empty Barrels
Ship Charles S. Whitney	New York (departed October 4) — Liverpool, England (arrived October 29)	11,541 Barrels Refined Oil
Ship Charles S. Whitney	Liverpool, England (departed November 30) — New York (arrived January 16, 1888)	Beer, Spirits, Salt, Iron Rails, Empty Barrels

1888

Captain Spicer went home from January until June 1888.

Ship Charles S. Whitney	New York (via Cape of Good Hope) (departed July 3) — Shanghai (arrived December 2)	66,117 Cases Refined Oil
Ship Charles S. Whitney	Shanghai (departed December 20) — Ilo Ilo, Philippines (arrived December 31)	Ballast

1889

Ship Charles S. Whitney	Ilo Ilo, Philippines (departed January 18) — Manila (arrived January 25)	1,651 Tons Sugar
Ship Charles S. Whitney	Manila (via Cape of Good Hope) (departed February 21) — New York (arrived June 16)	1,651 Tons Sugar, 6,500 Bales Hemp

Ship	Departed	Arrived	Cargo
Ship Charles S. Whitney	New York (departed July 25)	London (arrived August 19)	11,465 Barrels Refined Oil
Ship Charles S. Whitney	London (departed September 25)	New York (arrived October 24)	4,500 Casks Cement
Ship Charles S. Whitney	New York (via Cape of Good Hope) (departed November 20)	Shanghai (arrived April 23, 1890)	66,650 Cases Refined Oil

1890

Ship	Departed	Arrived	Cargo
Ship Charles S. Whitney	Shanghai (departed June 30)	Hong Kong (arrived July 20)	896 Bales Wool and Straw Braid
Ship Charles S. Whitney	Hong Kong (via Cape of Good Hope) (departed August 16)	New York (arrived January 12,1891)	896 Bales Wool and Straw Braid and 2,505 Tons Straw Braid and Pepper

1891

Captain Spicer returned home. New ship *Glooscap*, 1,734 gross tons, was launched August 5, 1891.

Ship	Departed	Arrived	Cargo
Ship Glooscap	Spencers Island (departed September 15)	Liverpool, England (arrived October 15)	Lumber
Ship Glooscap	Liverpool (under tow) (departed November 7)	Cardiff, Wales (arrived November 9)	Ballast

Ship Glooscap   Cardiff, Wales (departed December 18)   Capetown, South Africa (arrived February 11, 1892)   2,922 Tons Coal

1892

Ship Glooscap   Capetown, South Africa (departed March 12)   Taltal, Chile (arrived May 22)   Ballast

Ship Glooscap   Taltal, Chile (via Cape Horn) (departed June 22)   New York (arrived September 5)   21,158 Bags Nitrate

Captain Spicer returned home where his wife died of cancer in late October. He rejoined the ship January 26, 1893.

1893

Ship Glooscap   New York (via Cape of Good Hope) (departed March 13)   Melbourne, Australia (arrived June 18)   Case Oil and General Cargo

Ship Glooscap   Melbourne, Australia (via Cape Horn) (departed September 2)   London (arrived December 10)   Wool, Tallow, General Cargo

1894

Ship	Departed	Arrived	Cargo
Ship Glooscap	London (departed January 24)	New York (arrived March 12)	5,700 Casks Cement
Ship Glooscap	New York (via Cape of Good Hope) (departed April 30)	Newcastle, Australia (arrived August 2)	General Cargo
Ship Glooscap	Newcastle, Australia (departed September 7)	Manila (arrived October 30)	2,600 Tons Coal
Ship Glooscap	Manila (under tow) (departed December 14)	Ilo, Ilo, Philippines (arrived December 17)	Ballast

1895

Ship	Departed	Arrived	Cargo
Ship Glooscap	Ilo Ilo, Philippines (via Cape of Good Hope) (departed January 12)	Halifax, Nova Scotia (arrived April 29)	2,900 Tons Sugar

Captain Spicer went home for the rest of the year. His brother Johnson took the *Glooscap*.

1896

No Records Available

1897

Ship	Departed	Arrived	Cargo
Ship Glooscap	Halifax, Nova Scotia (departed March 13)	New York (arrived March 23)	Ballast

Vessel	Departed	Arrived	Cargo
Ship Glooscap	New York (via Cape of Good Hope) (departed April 21)	Melbourne, Australia (arrived July 30)	3,389 Tons Oil
Ship Glooscap	Melbourne, Australia (departed September 3)	Newcastle, Australia (arrived September 8)	Ballast
Ship Glooscap	Newcastle, Australia (departed October 16)	Manila (arrived December 7)	2,710 Tons Coal

1898

Vessel	Departed	Arrived	Cargo
Ship Glooscap	Manila (under tow) (departed January 15)	Ilo Ilo, Philippines (arrived January 17)	Ballast
Ship Glooscap	Ilo Ilo, Philippines (via Cape of Good Hope) (departed February 2)	Philadelphia (arrived May 22)	2,850 Tons Sugar
Ship Glooscap	Philadelphia (via Cape of Good Hope) (departed June 26)	Manila (arrived November 19)	3,000 Tons Coal

1899

Vessel	Departed	Arrived	Cargo
Ship Glooscap	Manila (under tow) (departed January 25)	Ilo Ilo, Philippines (arrived January 27)	Ballast
Ship Glooscap	Ilo Ilo, Philippines (via Cape of Good Hope) (departed March 28)	Philadelphia (arrived August 2)	3,800 Tons Sugar

	Departed	Arrived	Cargo
Ship Glooscap	Philadelphia (under tow) (departed August 18)	New York (arrived August 21)	Ballast. Vessel drydocked for repairs
Ship Glooscap	New York (under tow) (departed August 29)	Norfolk, Virginia (arrived August 30)	Ballast

Captain Spicer went home for the rest of the year while his brother Dewis took the *Glooscap*. He rejoined the ship in January 1900.

1900

	Departed	Arrived	Cargo
Ship Glooscap	New York (via Cape of Good Hope) (departed March 2)	Melbourne, Australia (arrived June 15)	Oil, Resin and Slate
Ship Glooscap	Melbourne, Australia (departed July 13)	Newcastle, Australia (arrived July 25)	Part cargo of Coal
Ship Glooscap	Newcastle, Australia (departed August 8)	Manila (arrived October 11)	3,790 Tons Coal
Ship Glooscap	Manila (departed December 10)	Tacoma, U.S.A. (arrived February 14, 1901)	Ballast

1901

	Departed	Arrived	Cargo
Ship Glooscap	Tacoma, U.S.A. (departed April 4)	Melbourne, Australia (arrived June 20)	Lumber and Shingles
Ship Glooscap	Melbourne, Australia (departed August 3)	Newcastle, Australia (arrived August 7)	415 Tons Iron Rails

Ship	Departed	Arrived	Cargo
Ship Glooscap	Newcastle, Australia (departed September 1)	Manila (arrived October 22)	2,681 Tons Coal
Ship Glooscap	Manila (departed December 7)	Singapore (arrived December 16)	Ballast. Vessel drydocked for repairs.

1902

Ship	Departed	Arrived	Cargo
Ship Glooscap	Singapore (via Cape of Good Hope) (departed March 11)	Boston (arrived June 24)	2,712 Tons Coffee, Tapioca and General Cargo. Only part* discharged.
Ship Glooscap	Boston (under tow) (departed July 2)	New York (arrived July 4)	Discharged rest* of Cargo.

Captain Spicer was on shore until July 1903 — part of the time home and part of the time in New York supervising repairs to the *Charles S. Whitney* which had been in a collision.

1903

Ship	Departed	Arrived	Cargo
Ship George T. Hay	New York (departed August 8)	Havre-Rouen, France (arrived September 5)	10,719 Barrels Oil
Ship George T. Hay	Rouen, France (departed October 10)	New York (arrived November 22)	1,230 Tons Chalk

1904

Captain Spicer spent most of 1904 in New York arranging charters for the various Spencers Island vessels. He was home for a rest and rejoined the *Glooscap* in January 1905.

1905

Ship Glooscap	New York (departed February 25)	Rosario, Argentina (arrived May 1)	Lumber, Wire, General Cargo
Ship Glooscap	Rosario, Argentina (departed July 1)	Rio de Janeiro, Brazil (arrived July 24)	2,547 Tons Hay
Ship Glooscap	Rio de Janeiro, Brazil (departed September 2)	Charleston, South Carolina (arrived October 17)	1,200 Bags Coffee
Ship Glooscap	Charleston, S.C. (departed November 7)	Boston (arrived November 14)	Ballast

1906

Ship Glooscap	Boston (departed January 17)	Buenos Aires, Argentina (arrived March 17)	Lumber
Ship Glooscap	Buenos Aires, Argentina (departed July 23)	New York (arrived September 26)	2,009 Tons Quebacho Wood

1907

Ship Glooscap	New York (departed February 11)	
Ship Glooscap	Rosario, Argentina (arrived April 23)	Lumber
Ship Glooscap	Rosario, Argentina (departed June 9)	
Ship Glooscap	Rio de Janeiro, Brazil (arrived June 26)	2,680 Tons Hay
Ship Glooscap	Rio de Janeiro, Brazil (departed August 3)	
Ship Glooscap	Port of Spain, Trinidad (arrived August 25)	Ballast
Ship Glooscap	Port of Spain, Trinidad (departed August 27)	
Ship Glooscap	La Brea, Trinidad (arrived August 27)	Ballast
Ship Glooscap	La Brea, Trinidad (departed October 1)	
Ship Glooscap	New York (arrived October 23)	2,270 Tons Pitch
Ship Glooscap	New York (under tow) (departed November 26)	
Ship Glooscap	Boston (arrived November 28)	Ballast

Captain Spicer went home until rejoining the *Glooscap* in Campbellton, N.B. in June 1908.

1908

Ship Glooscap	Campbellton, N.B. (departed July 18)	
Ship Glooscap	Rosario, Argentina (arrived September 26)	Lumber
Ship Glooscap	Rosario, Argentina (departed November 8)	
Ship Glooscap	Barbados (arrived December 25 for orders)	Ballast

127

1909

Ship	Departed	Arrived	Cargo
Ship Glooscap	Barbados (departed February 17)	Boston (arrived March 9)	Ballast
Ship Glooscap	Boston (departed April 11)	Buenos Aires, Argentina (arrived June 14)	Lumber
Ship Glooscap	Buenos Aires, Argentina (departed July 17)	Barbados (arrived August 21 for orders)	Ballast
Ship Glooscap	Barbados (departed September 7)	Sabine Pass, Texas (arrived October 2)	Ballast
Ship Glooscap	Sabine Pass, Texas (departed November 16)	Buenos Aires, Argentina (arrived January 19, 1910)	Lumber

1910

Ship	Departed	Arrived	Cargo
Ship Glooscap	Buenos Aires, Argentina (departed April 7)	Barbados (arrived May 11 for orders)	Ballast
Ship Glooscap	Barbados (departed May 16)	La Brea, Trinidad (arrived May 19)	Ballast
Ship Glooscap	La Brea, Trinidad (departed June 14)	New York (arrived July 1)	1,400 Tons Pitch

Selected Bibliography

American Bureau of Shipping. *Record of American and Foreign Shipping.* New York: Various Years.

Armour, Charles and Lackey, Thomas. *Sailing Ships of the Maritimes.* Toronto: McGraw-Hill Ryerson Ltd., 1975.

Byers, Conrad, ed. *The Best Of Our Parrsborough Shore Heritage.* Parrsboro: The Citizen, 1982.

Catton, Bruce. *Never Call Retreat.* New York: Doubleday and Company, Inc., 1965.

Chittick, Hattie. *Hantsport, The Smallest Town.* Kentville: Kentville Publishing Co., 1940.

Eaton, Arthur Wentworth. *The History of King's County, N.S.* Salem, Mass.: Salem Press, 1910.

Fay, Charles Edey, *Mary Celeste — The Odyssey of an Abandoned Ship.* Salem, Mass.: Peabody Museum, 1942.

Leckie, Robert. *The Wars of America.* New York: Harper and Row, 1968.

Lubbock, Basil. *The Colonial Clippers.* 4th ed. Glasgow: Brown, Son and Ferguson, 1948.

MacMechan, Archibald. *There Go the Ships.* Toronto: McClelland and Stewart, Ltd., 1928.

Monsarrat, Nicholas. *The Master Mariner.* London: Pan Books, 1979.

Mosher, Edith. *White Rock, The Story of Gypsum in Hants County.* Hantsport: Lancelot Press, 1979.

Parker, Captain John P. *Sails of the Maritimes.* Halifax: Maritime Museum of Canada, 1960.

Pohl, Frederick. *Prince Henry Sinclair.* New York: Clarkson N. Potter, Inc., 1974.

Spicer, Stanley T. *Masters of Sail.* Halifax: Petheric Press, 1982.

Sails of Fundy. Hantsport: Lancelot Press, 1979.

Villiers, Alan et al. *Men, Ships and the Sea.* Washington: National Geographic Society, 1962.

Wallace, Frederick William. *In the Wake of the Windships.* Toronto: Musson, 1927.

Record of Canadian Shipping, 1786-1920. Toronto: Musson, 1929.

Wooden Ships and Iron Men. Toronto: Hodder and Stoughton, 1923.

Williams, T. Harry et al. *A History of the United States Since 1865.* New York: Alfred A. Knopf, 1965.

Shipping Registers. Ports of Parrsboro and Windsor. Various years.